CONTENTS

LIBRARY OF CONGRESS
CATALOG CARD NO.: 79-67811

Meketa, C., etal
  One blanket and ten days' rations.

Globe, AZ: Southwest Parks and Monuments
Association

112 p.
8001   791003

ISBN 0911408-54-1

SOUTHWEST PARKS AND MONUMENTS ASSOCIATION
Box 1562—Globe, Arizona 85501

DEDICATION

To Ross R. Hopkins, Superintendent of Fort Union National Monument, to whom we, and the long deceased New Mexico Volunteers, owe a vote of thanks for his encouragement and assistance in telling their story.

In the field, meat and bread, and sugar and coffee, and salt, alone of all of the rations will be carried. One blanket apiece will be as much bedding as the men will be permitted to have when on a scout. To be encumbered with more is not to find Indians.

Brigadier General James Carleton, General Order 12, May 1, 1864

Foreword

The Chiricahua Apaches of southern Arizona were among the most formidable enemies the white men faced in their attempt to settle the West. Described by General George Crook, commander of the Department of Arizona, as the "tigers of the human race," the Chiricahuas were wily, brave, and determined. Aided by the harsh climate and rugged mountainous terrain of their traditional homeland, the Apaches bitterly fought not only the settlers and miners who invaded their territory but also the travelers who traversed the Butterfield Trail on their way to California. The years between 1860 and 1872 marked one of the bloodiest periods of Indian-Anglo warfare in Arizona. Early in the period Cochise and his people were fighting civilian encroachment on their lands but this soon became of secondary importance as they were faced with the problem of a military force which had been sent into the area to establish posts and supply depots; to furnish protective escorts to travelers; and to mount a campaign to track down and kill the Apaches in an attempt to crush their war-making powers.

Historians have credited U.S. Army troops and the California Volunteers with keeping the area at least partially safe during the 12 years Cochise waged open warfare against the white men. But little or no mention has been made of the contributions of two companies of New Mexico Infantry Volunteers who served in the Arizona Territory from June, 1864, until June, 1866. These companies, stationed at Fort Goodwin and Fort Bowie, were part of the Apache Expedition which was planned and executed by General James Carleton from his headquarters in Santa Fe in the spring and summer of 1864. Carleton, military commander of the New Mexico Territory which then included Arizona, believed, erroneously, that a swift, concentrated attack on the Apaches by a number of the military units under his command, bolstered by parties of miners who volunteered their services, and bands of Pima and Maricopa Indians, would overwhelm the Apaches and bring about their defeat quickly. Although his goal was not achieved, the New Mexicans did an admirable job during their service in Arizona.

The raising of a volunteer military force from the civil populace in New Mexico originally came about as a result of an invasion of the Territory by a small force of Texans in 1861. Circumstances allowed the Texans, under the command of Colonel John Baylor, quickly and easily to gain control of the southern region of New Mexico, which he designated as the Confederate Territory of Arizona. His success encouraged the Confederates to begin raising a large army in Texas to be used in a plan to invade and seize all the New Mexico Territory. If successful in marching up the Rio Grande and capturing both the capital at

v

Santa Fe and the major military post of Fort Union, the Confederates believed they could eventually control much of the West and be able, in time, to acquire much of the mineral wealth of the Colorado and California gold fields with which to finance the South's struggle.

Baylor's invasion caught New Mexico seriously undermanned, with few U.S. Army troops and no effective military force. Requests for assistance were dispatched to California and Colorado and immediate efforts begun to recruit volunteers from the native population. During the six months while the Texas army was being recruited and trained, the same activities were taking place in New Mexico. Eventually, five regiments of New Mexico infantry volunteers, some not at full strength, were enlisted.

This volunteer force, with a limited number of Regular Army troops, one company of Colorado men, and some untrained New Mexico militiamen, was unsuccessful in its first confrontation with the Confederates at the Battle of Valverde near Fort Craig, on the Rio Grande. However, in March, 1862, at Glorieta Pass in northern New Mexico, the Texans were defeated by a combined force of New Mexicans, Regular Army troops, and additional Colorado volunteers who had made a rugged march southward into the Territory through deep mountain snows just in time to meet the enemy. Disorganized and short of supplies, the Texans then retreated southward down the Rio Grande, pursued by the Union forces, and eventually left New Mexico.

Once the Confederate threat was dis-posed of, the Colorado troops returned to the north for duty against the Indians, most of the U.S. Army soldiers were sent East, and the New Mexico volunteer infantry units were deactivated. Many New Mexicans who had served in the infantry units, however, were transferred into a newly organized cavalry regiment under the command of Kit Carson. This single cavalry unit, along with a number of California volunteer troops which had arrived in the Territory in July, too late to fight the Texans, was to be the major military strength used in an effort to combat the various Indian tribes which had become particularly troublesome during the time military attention had been directed toward the Texans.

Carson's cavalry regiment began the roundup of Mescalero Apaches and Navajos while most of the California troops were assigned duties in the Arizona Territory and at various posts in New Mexico. It soon became apparent to the military headquarters in Santa Fe that the release of so many trained infantry volunteers had been premature and that more troops were now needed. Concentration of the bulk of the Territory's military manpower in the western sectors had left other areas sparsely protected and soon other tribes were taking advantage of the situation. To the north and east, the Plains Indians became so bold, with attacks against wagon trains along the Santa Fe Trail, that supplies were almost cut off and settlers in the area were forced to leave their homes. In the south, westward from the Rio Grande into Arizona, the southern Apaches of the Mimbres, Gila,

vi

Mogollon, and Chiricahua tribes had practically immobilized all attempts to settle, mine, or travel through the area.

In an attempt to raise more troops to cope with the problems, Henry Connelly, governor of New Mexico Territory, authorized reactivation of the First New Mexico Infantry Volunteers in September, 1863. Recruiting was begun, mainly in northern New Mexico where the bulk of the population was situated, and both veterans of earlier volunteer organizations and untested novices were enlisted. By June, 1864, the tenth and final company of the regiment had been manned and organized. General Carleton directed operations from his Santa Fe headquarters and deployed the infantry units in northeastern New Mexico, southward along the Rio Grande at various posts, and in southern Arizona.

The vast majority of New Mexico volunteer soldiers were Hispanics, unschooled laborers and farmers who spoke little English and were unfamiliar with standards and attitudes of the American military establishment in which they were serving. They made excellent soldiers, however, and were particularly suited for the service they were to see. For generations their families had lived in the Southwest and these men had acquired a vast store of practical knowledge about Indians and their ways which,

combined with their familiarity with the harsh and formidable terrain of the mountains and deserts of the area, gave them an advantage over Anglo soldiers who had arrived from other parts of the country. A review of military events in Arizona for the years 1864–1866 appears to show that Apaches recognized the skills of their long-time opponents and avoided confrontations with the New Mexicans, preferring instead to attack parties of California volunteer soldiers.

Two of the 10 companies of the reorganized infantry volunteers of New Mexicans were sent to serve in Arizona as part of General Carleton's Apache Expedition. This is their story. Company A was stationed, for 2 years, at the isolated Fort Bowie, guarding the vital Apache Pass and Company I helped establish Fort Goodwin, farther north in the valley of the Tularosa.

It would not be their lot to be involved in any spectacular battles or to gain fame or recognition. Instead they endured protracted hardships, toil, and privation of a nature which cannot be appreciated by anyone who has not experienced it. They exhibited a quiet courage made up of self-denial, perseverance, and strength of will until their tour of duty was completed and they were relieved by Regular Army troops in 1866.

COMPANY A

1st INFANTRY NEW MEXICO VOLUNTEERS

Company muster rolls show that recruiting for Company A was done, mostly in the Santa Fe area, by three men, Sergeant Candelario Martinez, First Lieutenant Henry W. Lauer, and Captain Nicolas Quintana.[1] In little more than a month, from September 21 to October 31, 1863, they enlisted a number of men and the company formed at Fort Marcy in the capital city. On November 22, Special Order No. 55 was issued from Headquarters, Department of New Mexico, which said:

> Captain Nicolas Quintana of the 1st Infantry, New Mexico Volunteers, having completed the organization of his Company A of that regiment, will take post with that Company at Fort Union, New Mexico, starting from Fort Marcy as soon as the Chief Quartermaster can furnish the necessary transportation. Colonel, 1st Infantry, N. M. Vols. will make the necessary estimates for the muskets and accoutrements to completely arm this company, so that no time may be lost in having it drilled and got ready for active service as soon as practicable after its arrival at Fort Union. Immediately upon the arrival of this Company at that post, Lieut. Colonel McMullen, Commanding at Fort Union will institute a rigid system of instruction and discipline for the Company; will have the officers and non-commissioned officers thoroughly instructed in the theory as well as practice of their duties; will have three recitations in Tactics per week, both for officers and noncommissioned officers; and will have the Company carefully drilled commencing at the School of the Soldier, at the earliest possible moment.[2]

Company A left Santa Fe on November 28 and arrived at Fort Union, 169 kilometers (105 miles) to the northeast, on December 4.[3] Despite the newness of the company, it was already to suffer the loss of a man. Private Jose Maria Romero, who had enlisted on October 12, became ill and was left behind at Fort Marcy. He never recovered and died there on December 20 of unknown causes. Lieutenant

Lauer also remained in Santa Fe until December 9, possibly to continue recruiting, and then traveled to the fort to rejoin the company. Records show that on his trip to Fort Union he escorted 35 Navajos, possibly prisoners captured by Kit Carson's troops, who were being transported to the Bosque Redondo reservation.

On January 18, 1864, Lieutenant Lauer and Sergeant Martinez were given permission to begin organization of a new company, to be designated Company B. Although they continued to be carried on the books as members of Company A, they left immediately for Santa Fe, where they once again involved themselves in recruiting duties. Their departure left Captain Quintana and a Lieutenant Juan Tapia as actual officers of Company A. By June, Lauer and Martinez had organized and activated Company B and were officially assigned to it with promotions to captain and second lieutenant, respectively.[4]

Two months after Company A arrived at Fort Union, Private Victorino Dominguez deserted on February 8. Desertions, always a problem in the military, began among the New Mexico Volunteers, most of whom were poorly educated natives, not fluent in English, who had been born into a culture whose values differed significantly from those of the eastern Americans who had established the military procedures and ethics under which they were serving. Dominguez was apprehended and put into confinement on April 15. He, like several other volunteer soldiers who had deserted, was sentenced to death at his General Court Martial.

Reportedly, in an effort to make examples of the deserters, a carefully-planned but pitiless bit of play acting was carried out on orders from Santa Fe headquarters. The standard execution process was begun and each of the deserters was marched out and positioned in front of a firing squad. Each step of the tense drama was carried out, right up to the point

3

where the order to fire was to be given and then, just at the moment the terrified prisoners expected to die, the proceedings were halted and the men given a reprieve. Then, General Order No. 30, dated September 21, 1864, which General Carleton had sent from his headquarters in Santa Fe, was read. The order said that the death sentences of Dominguez and two other deserters were to be "mitigated in each case to confinement with ball and chain at hard labor, in charge of the guard, at the posts where each of these soldiers is now confined, for a period of three years, without pay or allowances, and with only enough clothing for their absolute necessities."[5]

In Dominguez's case, a plea had been made that, because he was a Navajo, he hadn't really understood what he was doing when he deserted and had been unaware of its serious consequences. In his order remitting the men to prison, Carleton said that this plea had affected his decision for clemency and that the men would be given "the benefit of the doubt ... as to their knowledge of the penalty due to this crime." He did, however, severely castigate them, saying, "They basely perjured themselves, shamefully deserted their flag, and have fairly forfeited their lives by the laws of their country, and by the sentence of a Court."

Carleton made it amply clear that he did not intend to be equally generous in the future. The order continued:

This order will be read upon parade at each post within the Department every Sunday evening for a period of six weeks; and, at posts where soldiers of the New Mexican regiments are serving, it will be read in the Spanish language. After that period shall have expired, let it be well remembered, that no clemency need be asked for, nor expected, by any officer or soldier who shall be legally convicted of having deserted the service, and been sentenced to forfeit his life for so heinous a crime.

Dominguez, however, was not to serve the entire three-year sentence. On April 24, 1865, General Order No. 1 was issued from military headquarters in Santa Fe extending a general amnesty to all military prisoners, regardless of their crimes. The amnesty was issued in honor of the capture of Richmond and Petersburg in Virginia and directed that all prisoners be released and returned to duty. It stipulated that the men would have to make up time owed, and pay any fines due, but also stated that those who had been sentenced to be drummed out would be restored to duty and all those whose pay had been stopped would have it started again.

On May 10, as a result of the amnesty order, Dominguez was released from imprisonment after having served only about 7½ months, and allowed to go back on duty as a private with Company A. He served the remainder of his enlistment without further incident and was honorably discharged on September 26, 1866, with the rest of the men of the company.

Even though, at the time of Dominguez's desertion, the men of Company A were supposed to be undergoing military training, in reality, they were assigned many other duties. The soldiers were used for building and repair work being done on Fort Union, were sent out on guard details to escort mail and supply wagons on short trips in the vicinity, and did provost guard duty at Loma Parda, 9 kilometers (6 miles) southwest of the fort.

The town, whose name translates to Gray Hill, was a favorite spot for off-duty soldiers from the fort and was filled with gambling houses, saloons, and dance halls. Naturally, violence often erupted and drunken brawls were not uncommon. On April 29, 1864, Company A lost Private Olayio Tarin who had been shot earlier while carrying out provost duty in the town and died at Fort Union from his wounds.

While the men of Company A were busy

4

with their training and other duties at Fort Union, events were occurring in Arizona and Santa Fe which would soon affect them. General Carleton had decided to mount a campaign against the hostile Apaches in southwestern New Mexico and southern Arizona. His plans included use of some New Mexico infantry volunteers. On April 18, 1864, orders were issued by Carleton in Santa Fe and sent to Captain Quintana at Fort Union in which both Company A and Company I of the volunteers were told to be prepared at all points for active field service.[6] They were ordered to proceed, as a battalion, without delay, to Las Cruces, New Mexico. From that post they would be sent westward to Arizona as part of Carleton's Apache Expedition. The orders stated each company would be provided with 20,000 rounds of ammuntion suited to the caliber of the muskets with which their regiment was armed. Carleton, with a background as a Regular Army officer, appeared to be prejudiced against native troops, frequently expressing dissatisfaction with volunteers for their failure to measure up to his standards for proper soldiering. He ended the routine orders with a rather sarcastic comment urging the units to display a military manner, saying, "Let it be seen with what good order these troops of a new regiment can be marched through their native Territory."

The men left Fort Union on May 7. Their march was to be by way of Galisteo, San Antonio, Los Pinos, and Fort Craig. This route required the troops to march southwest from Fort Union until they could pass through Tijeras Canyon near Albuquerque and make their way to the Rio Grande River. Once the river had been reached the troops would march southward to Los Pinos, Governor Connelly's ranch, which was being rented by the military as a camp. After a brief stopover there, the unit was to continue south. However, company returns for May, 1864, show that a dramatic incident took place shortly after their departure from the Connelly hacienda.

Before the two New Mexico companies left Fort Union, all their personnel then in the fort guardhouse had been ordered released to custody of company commanders. These men, who had been incarcerated for various crimes, were being transported with their units on the trip south. Upon arrival at Las Cruces, prisoners under detention were to be turned over to the commander of the guard at that post. Company A was transporting several such men and, on May 22, near Belen, two apparently attempted escape. Corporal Agapita Ortiz, in charge of the battalion guard, shot and killed Private Mauricio Silva. The musket ball he fired glanced off Silva and wounded Private Nasario Crespin in the left leg. Both men were under confinement for desertion.[7]

Silva had deserted while the company was at Fort Union, after only 2 month's service. Crespin, however, apparently had been trying to outwit the military, possibly to obtain several of the enlistment bonuses offered to recruits. He had enlisted in Company A, in Santa Fe, just 5 days before they were to leave for Fort Union. Then, 13 days later, two days after arrival at Fort Union, he deserted on December 6, 1863. A month later he reappeared in Santa Fe and joined Company C which was in the process of signing up men. Unfortunately for Crespin, by February 29, 1864, his deception had been discovered and he was returned to Company A as a deserter. After being wounded in the escape attempt, Crespin was transported, with the company, to Fort Craig, where he was left in the hospital. There he was eventually court marshalled and drummed out of the service in September.

After the incident, the company continued southward along the river and reached Las Cruces on June 4, completing 646 kilometers (400-mile) march from Fort Union. The men were given little time to rest; on the day of their

5

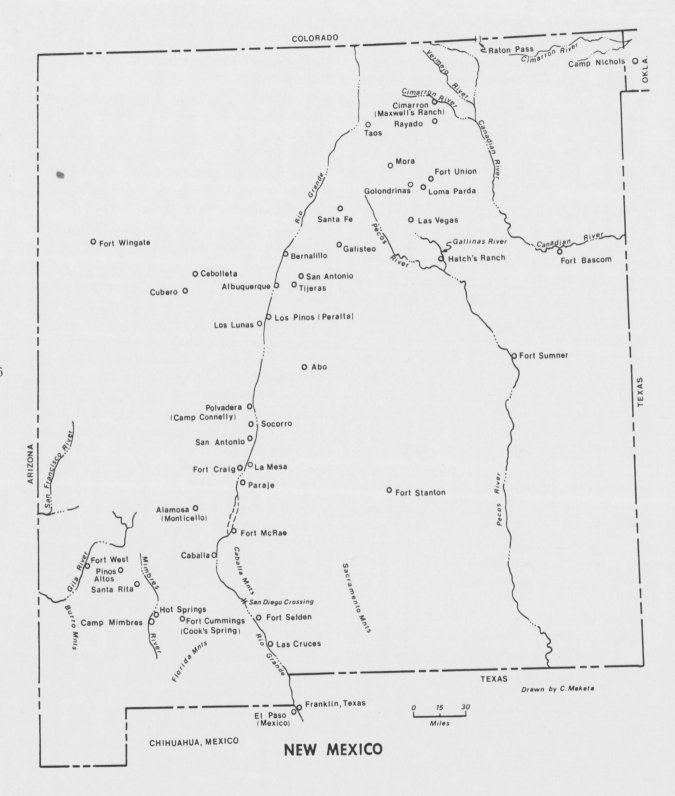

6

Drawn by C. Meketa

NEW MEXICO

arrival at this rendezvous point for the Apache Expedition, an order was issued appointing Major Thomas Blakeney, of the First California Cavalry, as commander of the battalion for its march west to Arizona.[8] The two New Mexico companies were told to be ready to march at noon on June 8, taking rations to last them until the 25th of the month and 100 rounds of ammunition for each man, 40 of which they would carry in cartridge boxes and 60 in the wagons.

The two companies traveled westward together until they reached a camp site, either in western New Mexico or eastern Arizona, named Cienaga. The exact location of this watering hole is not known, but there they split up. Company A had been posted to Fort Bowie as part of the post garrison, while Company I was to join the main force of the Apache Expedition at Fort Goodwin. At the time of separation, 11 men from Company I were detailed to escort the men of A Company to their destination. Then they, under command of a sergeant of the California Infantry Volunteers, would bring back the wagons used to transport the Company A supplies to Fort Bowie.[9]

At daylight, on June 18, after their 290 kilometer (180-mile) trek from Las Cruces, the weary men of Company A caught their first sight of Fort Bowie, which was to be their home for the next 2 years.[10] It could hardly have been a reassuring sight with its few crude structures and its isolated position; to make matters worse, Company A was seriously under strength, with only two officers and 54 men. In an effort to alleviate the personnel shortage, Company A would continue recruiting efforts throughout the entire time they were stationed in the area. It was standard policy of the New Mexico Volunteers, who were perennially short of men, to carry on recruiting practices wherever they were stationed, regardless of the activities in which involved. Official records show that a number of men were mustered in at both

Tubac and Tucson, two supply depots in the area, to bolster the strength of Company A over the next several years.

Fort Bowie, Company A's new duty post, had been established in 1862 at Apache Pass in southeastern Arizona, at the site of a spring that was an unfailing source of water. This was the homeland of the Chiricahua Apaches. There had been bloodshed and enmity between them and the white men since a late 1860 confrontation between an Army lieutenant and Cochise, the Apache leader, over a theft of livestock and kidnapping of a Mexican boy at a nearby ranch. On his march east to aid the New Mexicans in 1862, General Carleton's troops had battled the Apaches at the spot and he ordered a fort built in an effort to keep the pass open to travelers and soldiers.

Life at Fort Bowie, at the time Company A was stationed there, was primitive. The post was isolated, the quarters rude, the food bad, and sickness prevalent.[11] Although Indians were seldom seen in the immediate vicinity, they were nonetheless present in the surrounding hills, and vigilance was always necessary. Duty there followed the same pattern as at the other camps, with reveille at daylight, drill until breakfast at 7 a.m., and work throughout the day until taps were sounded at 9 p.m. Sunday inspections were held at 6:30 a.m. and orders stated that all arms on the post were to be kept clean but unloaded with exception of those carried by men on guard duty, which were always ready for use. Men coming off guard duty would each be allowed one shot at a target and the man whose aim had been best was excused from his next guard duty. The men lived in tents inside stone breastworks on a commanding hill above the spring. It would not be until 1866, when regular army troops replaced the volunteers, that a new post of conventional buildings would be constructed.

That June of 1864, when Company A arrived at Fort Bowie, Company K of the Fifth

7

8

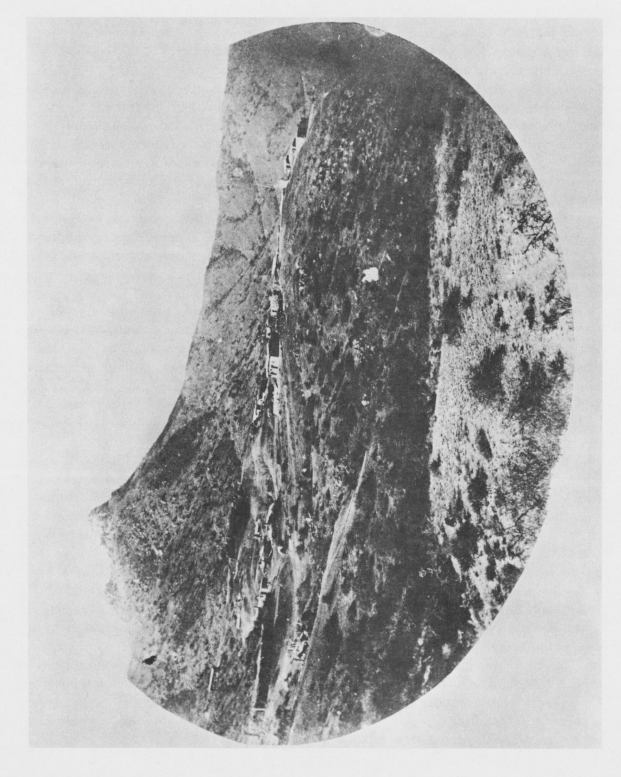

First Fort Bowie, ca. 1867
Courtesy of the Arizona Historical Society

Infantry, California Volunteers and a detachment of Company E of the First California Cavalry, all under the command of Captain Thomas T. Tidball, were already stationed there.[12] They, however, were soon to leave, and Company A apparently was their replacement. For the next several months, while New Mexico and California infantrymen jointly occupied the fort, average troop strength appeared to be approximately five officers and 130 enlisted men for the post.[13]

That summer, however, the 3-year enlistment period for the California volunteers was expiring, for they had been recruited in 1861 after onset of the Civil War. Aware of this, General Carleton ordered a number of reorganizations in the Arizona area during July, including evacuation and closing of Tucson as a military post and the movement of supplies to other installations, including Fort Bowie.[14] Once this had been done, the California troops were ordered to proceed to Las Cruces, New Mexico,

to be mustered out of service there on the proper day. In seems curious that Carleton would have initiated his Apache Expedition that summer, given the fact that he was about to lose troop strength with the departure of many California men who had been active in the area, but nonetheless, he did.

By August, Captain Tidball and his men had left, presumably for Las Cruces, and the New Mexico infantrymen remained as the only unit to handle both the operations of the fort and expeditions against the Indians. For the next 4 months, from September through December, 1864, the post was operated with an average of only 77 enlisted men, resulting in great hardship for the soldiers.[15] Since Company A was not to be assigned another officer until the end of December, Captain Quintana was required to handle matters at the fort and Second Lieutenant Tapia was needed to be out in the field most of the time.

Conditions were miserable. The post was

9

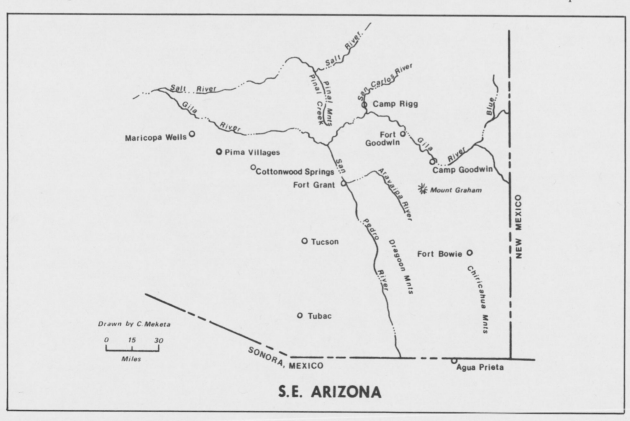

S.E. ARIZONA

isolated and in an area described as one of the two most dangerous spots in the southwestern New Mexico and southeastern Arizona territory. In his official report, written in October, 1863, Captain Tidball said that Fort Bowie was an unhealthy spot with quarters that were mere hovels, mostly excavations in the side of a hill.[16] He described them as damp and ill-ventilated. Captain Quintana and Lieutenant Tapia both suffered consequences of prolonged overwork and deplorable living conditions. By early January, 1865, Tapia was so sick he had to be relieved of his duties and by February 11, of the same year, Captain Quintana was sent to Las Cruces on sick leave at a doctor's recommendation. Although Quintana continued to be carried on official roles as a captain of Company A, there is no documentation to show that he ever returned to the post. It was Lieutenant Tapia, however, who suffered the most severe consequences resulting from duty at Fort Bowie, for they eventually led to his death.

That summer of 1864, when the troops of Company A first arrived at Fort Bowie, they were quickly put to work. Less than a month after the company's arrival, Lieutenant Tapia and 25 men from A went out on an Apache scout with 32 California infantry volunteers. The party was under the command of Captain T. T. Tidball, the California volunteer officer, and was accompanied by a guide named Merejildo Grijalva. The scouting party was in the field from July 10 until August 1, looking for Apaches in the ravine-filled mountains which offered thousands of hiding places for the wily Indians. This was an introduction for the New Mexicans to the tactics used and hardships encountered in pursuit of Apaches in their own territory.[17] It was extremely rugged duty, for General Carleton expected the units to be highly mobile and had decreed that men in the field could carry no food other than meat, bread, sugar, coffee, and salt. He allowed them only one blanket apiece for bedding, and

justified this spartan regime by saying, "To be encumbered with more is not to find Indians."[18] While such an order may have seemed appropriate and bravely self-sacrificing when issued from the comfort of Carleton's Santa Fe headquarters, it surely took its toll on the health of men in the field. On this limited diet, and forced to drink whatever water they could find, even brackish, the infantrymen in Arizona covered long distances on foot, for periods up to a month, with only pack mules to carry their supplies.

Excerpts from Captain Tidball's report of the scout, which appeared in the *Santa Fe Weekly Gazette* of October 15, 1864, reveal many events and hardships the Company A men experienced. The party marched southeast from Fort Bowie, entered and explored all the deep canyons on the western slope of the Chiricahua Mountains, then marched southwest almost to the Mexican border. They arrived at the San Pedro River and marched downstream until they came to the Dragoon Mountains, scouted some canyons there, and eventually turned east once more and returned to Fort Bowie. The scouting party was in the field for 23 days and marched something over 483 kilometers (300 miles).

Bad weather plagued the troops from the onset of the scout, with frequent heavy rains in the mountains which sometimes limited visibility and often soaked the men and equipment, causing hardship and discomfort. On one occasion, a heavy thunderstorm didn't commence until they had stopped to make camp. By stretching their blankets over a framework of willow rods stuck in the ground and bent and fastened together at the top, the troops managed to keep dry during a 4-hour downpour. Paradoxically, on other occasions, the soldiers had great difficulty in finding good drinking water and had to dig in the sand in arroyo beds or obtain it from holes in rocks which held rain water.

On the second day of the scout, Captain Tidball found a canyon with permanent water and a large body of pine trees which he believed could supply all the timber and lumber required for building the contemplated new post at Apache Pass. He reported that the lumber could be transported over an excellent natural road and the distance would not exceed 25 miles. Later, as building began at Bowie, a lumber camp would be set up at the site.

By July 14 the party had climbed a very rough and exceedingly steep trail to reach a high, sharp divide, from the summit of which they could see, to the north, Dos Cabezas Mountains and Apache Pass. From there they made their way down to a spot called "Potrero," or pasture land, where they found an open grove of pine and fir trees, several springs of ice cold water, wild strawberries, gooseberries, wild potatoes and onions, and the whole region covered with nutritious grass. Tidball, surprised to find no evidence of Indians in such a lush place, asked the guide about their absence. Grijalva explained that Apaches avoided the spot because of the abundance of bears in the area.

Next morning the scouting party left the Potrero at 7 a.m. headed toward the Rio Ancho. It began raining shortly after the departure and continued without abating, so about 1 o'clock in the afternoon they made camp. Perhaps an hour later a guard, who had been posted, discovered several Indians climbing up a steep mountain approximately a mile from camp. A party of 21 soldiers was dispatched in pursuit immediately and when they had climbed to the area where the Indians had been seen they were hailed, in Spanish, by an Indian who was standing on an almost perpendicular cliff about 161 kilometers (100 feet) above them. The Indian shouted that he was a warrior and a brave one and commenced shooting arrows. When the arrows failed to inflict any damage he began to throw rocks, severely

bruising the arms of a California volunteer. The troops were firing at him and he soon fell, mortally wounded, and then called for Grijalva, whom he had recognized.

When the guide was satisfied that the Apache could no longer use his bow and arrows, he approached the downed man and tried to get him to talk, but the Indian would say nothing and soon died. Grijalva said he recognized the warrior as an Apache chief named Old Plume, one of Cochise's old warriors. Grijalva described him as an Indian guilty of numerous murders and robberies, sullen and tyrannical among his own people and merciless to all others.

Captain Tidball stated that Old Plume could easily have made his escape and speculated that the chief had either halted to cover the retreat of his women and children, or else considered it unworthy of a brave chief to run, and with savage stoicism had determined to sacrifice himself. Tidball said that in either case it was an act of heroism worthy of admiration, "even in an Apache." The troops pushed rapidly up the mountain in pursuit of the other Apaches but could not overtake them. They did find five jacals and several springs on the side of the mountain near the summit, from which they could see in all directions, and concluded it would have been impossible to surprise an Indian in that location.

The troops broke camp early next morning but had only traveled about 6.4 kilometers (4 miles) when they heard Indians hallooing from the cliffs. Captain Tidball sent Grijalva to talk to the Apaches and tell them to come into camp and make a treaty. While the troops waited, the guide and the Indians parlayed for 4 hours and finally four Apaches came down to the edge of a grove of trees about 1.6 kilometer (a mile) from the soldiers. One finally advanced to have a talk but refused to come too near. He said some members of the group belonged to Mangas' band and the rest to Cochise's band

and stated that they would come to the fort in 8 days to make a treaty. The cautious Indians refused to get close to the troops and when soldiers tried to overtake them they found it was useless. After their escape, the Apaches built signal fires along the cliffs in the direction the troops were moving, a sure sign there were other Indians ahead. Three days later, on July 18, Tidball tried a tactic which he hoped would surprise the Indians, at a rancheria near the Rio Ancho. At daybreak he sent Lieutenant Tapia, with the main force and pack trains, to proceed leisurely down the trail toward an old camp on the river, hoping they would act as decoys and attract the Indians' attention while he took Grijalva and 20 hand-picked men from his company over the nearly impassable mountain. The ploy, however, was unsuccessful, and when Tidball and his men arrived at the rancheria the Indians were gone.

The Apaches had apparently kept the troops under surveillance for the entire time they were on the scout and enjoyed taunting them. On July 21, the scouting party became aware that two Indians were following on horseback. Grijalva, the guide, was sent out to talk to them. He was well known to the Indians for he had been captured by the Chiricahuas in Sonora, Mexico, in 1853, and later, after regaining his freedom, had become a guide for Fort Bowie. The two Indians refused to come near the guide until he returned to the camp and left his musket. Finally one of the Apaches, Ka-eet-sah, who was an old acquaintance of Grijalva, came down to talk, while the other remained back to act as a lookout. Ka-eet-sah said there were no Indians in the mountains except for one small band with him and another small band at Rio Ancho and that the Mexicans had made a treaty with them at Fronteras and then broken it and killed about 30 members of the band.

Then Ka-eet-sah guilefully asked why the troops had gone back to the old camp, refer-

ring to the attempted decoy tactic initiated by Captain Tidball. With equal guile, Grijalva replied that the purpose had been to send word to Fort Bowie that the Indians would be coming in within 8 days, as they had promised, and to receive them kindly. The little game of wits continued with Grijalva asking the Apache why the nearby spring had dried up and the Apache answering "so that the soldiers could not follow the Indians" although he later gave the cause as lack of rain in the area for 2 years. Ka-eet-sah finally agreed to come into camp but told Grijalva that he wanted to smoke first. Grijalva gave the Apache some tobacco and went back to report his success. Ka-eet-sah had his smoke, then jumped on his horse and rode off rapidly. The outwitted Grijalva was furious with Captain Tidball because he hadn't tried to shoot the deceitful Indians.

After this incident the troops spent another 4 days in the mountains and found some trails that went to Fronteras, Mexico. On one trail they found tracks of a large band of cattle, mules, and burros which were less than 48 hours old, but did not follow them because they figured the infantrymen would not be able to catch up to the Indians and stock. In the vicinity they also found signs that a very large band of Indians had wintered over at that spot. The rest of the scout passed without incident.

Captain Tidball reported he did not believe a successful expedition could be made against the few Apaches who were in the Chiricahuas during the summer since they broke up into small bands with the approach of warm weather, living by plunder rather than cultivation of crops, and using mescal as the main staple of their diet. He felt it would be better to hunt them in winter when they banded into larger groups.

Tidball described the guide, Merejildo Grijalva, as a man thoroughly acquainted with the Chiricahua Mountains and familiar with the habits of the Indians but said he was con-

Merejildo Grijalva, scout and guide.
From the collection of the University of Arizona Library.

stitutionally timid, knowing as he did, the terrible fate awaiting him if ever captured by the Apaches. Captain Tidball said that Grijalva would not venture out of the sight of the soldiers and if he was compelled to go allowed his fears to overcome his judgement and his regard for the truth. Tidball suggested that, in company with another good scout, Grijalva would be very useful and that every expedition should have two or more scouts—one to follow the trail and the other to accompany him and watch the indications outside the trail, to prevent ambush and detect the presence of Indians.

Common sense dictates that the men of Company A carried out many more duties, including escort services and Indian patrols, than the fragmentary documents now available show. For example, Privates Ramon Martin, Canuto Gallegos, and Ignacio Roibal are listed as members of a group that traveled to Franklin, Texas, (now El Paso), on August 25, 1864, yet no further information is available about who was in charge or how many men accompanied them. On August 11, Private Hilario Gallegos had deserted while on an escort to Tucson, but no other details are given. Post returns do show, however, that Tapia left Bowie again on September 24, with some troops, to escort government wagons on a 290 kilometer (180-mile) trip to Las Cruces. While in Las Cruces, Tapia was promoted to first lieutenant. He returned to Fort Bowie on October 27 and, within a few days, on November 7, was sent out again, with a detail which included Private Jesus Ochoa (a native of Sonora, Mexico, who had enlisted at the fort only a month earlier) on an Apache scouting detail. After Tapia's return, he was ordered to leave again on December 14, with nine men, to make a trip to Las Cruces once more, from which they would not return until January 11, 1865.[19] On the same date, December 14, another escort, including Private Candelario Martin, left

for Tucson. During Tapia's absence, Captain Quintana gained some relief with the arrival of Second Lieutenant Thomas Coghlan, who became part of Company A on December 28, 1864.

Also during that December a request was sent to General Carleton's headquarters from Las Cruces that Company A be armed with the current model Springfield muskets to replace their outdated and less efficient caliber .69 smoothbore muskets.[20] In 1842 a .69 caliber smoothbore musket was adopted for general use. Also, from this time period until the Civil War a large number of Model 1822 to 1840 flintlock smoothbores were converted to percussion and they then closely resembled the Model 1842s. Company A weapons were undoubtedly from these arms. No documentation has been found to show whether or not the request was ever honored, but 6 months later, Colonel Abreu, commander of the New Mexico Infantry Volunteers, was still complaining from Fort Union that his regiment needed better arms in the form of the Springfield Rifle-musket.[21]

On January 12, 1865, Lieutenant Colonel Clarence E. Bennett of the First Cavalry, California Volunteers, arrived to oversee construction of some improved structures at Fort Bowie.[22] He remained at Bowie for only 6 months but during that time served as post commander, based on his superior rank. He was assisted by Captain G. C. Smith, Quartermaster, U.S. Volunteers, who had arrived 2 months before.[23] This additional duty of post construction would put an added burden on the men of Company A, even though troop strength at the fort was bolstered, from February through May, by the assignment of 15 California cavalrymen who were attached to Bowie.

Colonel Bennett, in a letter he sent to the Chief Quartermaster in Santa Fe, described Fort Bowie and cited "the absolute necessity for

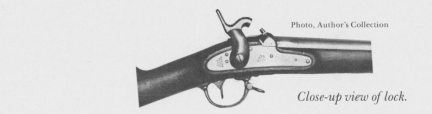

U.S. MUSKET, MODEL 1842   *Caliber .69 smoothbore*

Photo, Author's Collection

Close-up view of lock.

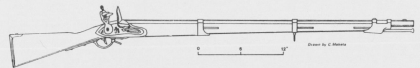

U.S. MUSKET MODEL 1822   *Caliber .69 smoothbore*

TYPICAL METHODS OF ALTERING FLINTLOCKS TO PERCUSSION SYSTEM

15

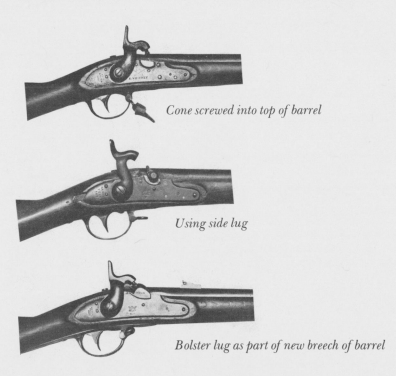

Cone screwed into top of barrel

Using side lug

Bolster lug as part of new breech of barrel

U. S. Model 1882 to 1840 flintlock muskets were converted by removing the flint mechanism and substituting a new hammer and cone. When converted, as shown, the muskets closely resembled the Model 1842 muskets.   Photos from Author's Collection

CARTRIDGES Caliber .69
(For use in smoothbore muskets)

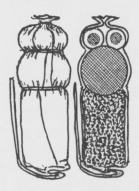

BALL   BUCK and BALL

Cartridge	528.01 gr.
Ball	432.9 gr.
Powder	75.0 gr.

Cartridge	662.36 gr.
Ball	432.9 gr.
3 Buckshot	129.03 gr.
Powder	75.0 gr.

16

NOTE: The caliber .69 smoothbore muskets used a round ball or a round ball and three buckshot called "Buck and Ball." This load was effective up to approximately 200 yards. These cartridges were wrapped in paper to contain all components and to serve as a "patch" for the ball

U.S. RIFLE-MUSKET, MODEL 1855
Caliber .58

Photo, Author's Collection

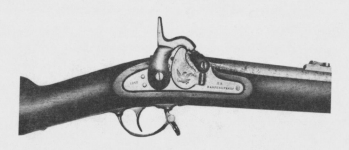

Close up view of musket showing "Maynard priming device." This is the Springfield Rifle-musket Company A was attempting to obtain.

speedily constructing suitable quarters for the troops guarding this (Apache) pass."[24] He said that the huts, which Captain Tidball had described 2 years earlier as mere hovels, were worse by the time he arrived. He said, "We have just had a long, terrific mountain storm. These huts presented truly a most wretched appearance. Those used by the officers were no better than those occupied by the men, as far as leaking was concerned. Repairing these quarters is out of the question, therefore, new ones should be constructed as speedily as possible..."

Colonel Bennett went on to cite a shortage of men to do the work, explaining, "There are only about men enough for two guards in addition to cut and haul fuel and hay and haul water. Escort duty and other work about the post makes duty very hard on this garrison, and, in addition, to expect them to build a post is truly a great expectation." Colonel Bennett requested that Company I be sent from Fort Goodwin to assist in the work, but Santa Fe never approved the request. Shorthanded as it was, Company A was expected to make the sacrifice and get the job done somehow.

During January, according to post returns, five enlisted men of Company A were sent on escort service to Tubac with Captain Smith, and on January 15, 1865, only 4 days after his return from the long trip to Las Cruces, Lieutenant Tapia, with one noncommissioned officer and 15 privates, was ordered to "proceed without delay to the timber about thirty miles from this Post and establish a lumber camp under the direction of Captain G. C. Smith, to construct sawpits and vigorously commence the work of getting out the timber and lumber required to construct Fort Bowie."[25] The order further instructed, "Lt. Tapia will report to the Commanding Officer at the end of the month the amount of work performed each day..."

Tapia marched to the lumber camp and his men set to work. But by early February word reached the fort that he was ill, and on February 6, Sergeant Mariano Sena, who had seen prior service with the New Mexico Militia in 1862, was ordered to the sawpit to relieve him from duty so that Tapia could return to the fort.[26]

Records for the next few months are sparse. They do show, however, that in February, Sergeant Dolores Anaya and 14 privates, along with six privates of the California troops, were sent to escort Paymaster S. C. Staples to Fort Goodwin.[27] On February 11, Captain Quintana, ill and on the recommendation of the doctor, left for Las Cruces, and with Lieutenant Tapia also sick and confined to bed in his quarters, the duties of commanding Company A fell on the shoulders of newly arrived Second Lieutenant Thomas Coghlan.

On March 5, 12 men from Company A were detailed to escort the paymaster to Tubac and three days later, since the work at the lumber camp was done, one corporal and four privates from the company were sent there to haul in the last load of lumber and all the cutting and sawing equipment to the post.[28] That month Colonel Bennett reported discovery of Indian tracks in Apache Pass and that examination showed them to be those of a reconnoitering party which had come to observe the post and the herds.[29] Fearful that the Indians intended to ambush and capture the post's herd, Bennett sent several scouting parties out but they found no Indians. Bennett stated, "I have fourteen armed men with the herd daily. The Indians cannot get anything here without a fight. The fight can be had at any time, but not the stock."

Tense and alert, the men of the post remained vigilant for any sign that Apaches might infiltrate the herd and make off with some animals. Only 1 day after Colonel Bennett had written the letter, the alarm was sounded at midnight. A guard, observing some light and hearing some noises outside the fort, gave warning, and the entire command was

17

View of Chiricahua Mountains
Ft. Bowie ruins in foreground ca. 1927
Courtesy Arizona Historical Society

18

roused. The soldiers, armed and ready for a fight, slipped outside the post under cover of darkness and stealthily made their way to the point from which the alerting noises had come. A human figure was seen and the men rushed forward and captured the culprit. Chagrined, they found not an Apache as expected, but one of their own. Corporal Santiago Gallegos of Company A, with incredibly bad timing, and for some private purpose known only to himself, had left the post without permission. Colonel Bennett, justifiably enraged, ordered Gallegos reduced to the rank of private, subject to the approval of his regimental commander, and confined to the guard house. The incident cost Gallegos dearly, for he never regained his rank, and a year and a half later, when he was discharged, he was still a private.[30]

On April 25, 10 New Mexico men were sent to Fort Cummings to escort subsistence stores to that post.[31] Records show that on April 26, Private Jose Martin was part of an escort party sent to Tucson. That there was much more activity than the records reveal

seems certain, for movement of the officers away from the post on various trips and detached service left Second Lieutenant Coghlan in charge as post commander in May, 1865. Colonel Bennett was at Tubac checking out subsistence stores available to supply Fort Goodwin until more supplies could be forwarded from California. Lieutenant Tapia still lay ill in his quarters and had been assigned Private Antonio Padilla, of the company, as a servant but was required to pay the government Padilla's salary. Captain Quintana and Quartermaster Smith were away, and so it fell to Coghlan, as post commander, to announce the assassination of President Lincoln to the troops on May 13, almost a month after the President's death.[32] Although word had been slow in reaching them, the flag was flown at the traditional half-mast for 30 days at the lonely outpost.

Company L of the California cavalry volunteers, with several officers and 68 enlisted men, arrived at Fort Bowie in late June, finally bolstering post strength to approximately 150 men. The two units would work together throughout the balance of Company A's tour there.

On July 10, Colonel Bennett left Fort Bowie with 12 California cavalrymen to examine and report on a wagon road that led to Maricopa Wells, a 341 kilometer (212-mile) trip. His report on the expedition gave much insight into conditions in that portion of Arizona, an area through which the men of Company A often had to travel.[33] He described the extreme heat, areas of deep sand which made travel difficult, exhaustion of the mules and horses, and the problems with finding water. In one instance he noted that it "rained hard, furnishing water in rocks for men and animals" and on another he noted that after a 5.6 kilometer (3.5 mile) struggle down a canyon, through the very heaviest sand under terrible heat, he and his men "found water stagnant, green, strong of alkali, and unfit for man or beast. Cleaned out the water holes and waited from 1 to 5 p.m. for water to drizzle in. Got three-fourths of a bucket of water for each of the mules, none for the horses ..." Near Fort Bowie he mentioned fresh tracks of Indians "of twelve or thirteen bucks on one trail" and later, near the San Pedro River, the party found the trail of a war party of nearly 100, which their guide, Lojinio, said had killed someone and could possibly attack them. Bennett used every precaution against the Indians, camping early to finish the cooking so the fires could all be put out before dark and ordering that all "carbines, pistols, and ammunition were put every night in readiness for a fight before morning." He said that, "considering the Indian trails I passed, the numerous Indian tracks, indicating the close proximity of large numbers of Indians, in getting through safe I consider I did very well."

Back at Fort Bowie, during that month, other incidents were occurring. On the evening of July 3, Corporal Agapito Ortiz once again received official attention. He was the same noncommissioned officer who had shot the two deserters who attempted to escape the previous May near Belen. Apparently, at the time of the shooting incident, Captain Quintana had detoured to Santa Fe and was not with his men, so Captain Simpson of Company I was in charge of both companies. For some reason which has never been uncovered, Captain Simpson preferred a charge of murder against Corporal Ortiz for the prisoner shooting and sent it to Santa Fe. Possibly Ortiz had been careless in some way which allowed the two prisoners to make their attempt to flee. By the time official action had been taken on the matter, Company A was already at Fort Bowie and it was there that the word was received to have Ortiz arrested and put in irons under heavy guard in June, 1864. However the matter was finally resolved, Ortiz apparently retained his rank but now, a year later, was arrested for being drunk and unable to perform his duties as commander of the main guard. This time he was reduced in rank to private, a rank he held until his discharge.[34]

On July 11, an order was issued that another lumber camp was to be established at Ajo del Carrizo, about 32 kilometers (20 miles) from the fort, and 20 men from Company A were sent there to work, under the command of a California cavalry sergeant.[35] Again, the lumber was to be used for fort construction. These men were relieved by another detail sent from the fort on August 31.[36]

On July 25, funeral ceremonies were held for a 28-year-old private, Vivian Lucero, who had enlisted in Las Cruces just 6 months earlier. The troops were ordered to parade, with side arms, at 2 p.m., and the firing party was composed of Corporal Jose Pena and eight privates from Company A.[37]

On August 18, Captain Quintana, who apparently had never returned from Las Cruces, was promoted to major and assigned to regimental duties at Fort Union. This loss of their

19

commanding officer meant little to the men at Fort Bowie, since no replacement for Quintana would arrive for months and although Tapia was still carried on the books as a company officer, he lay critically ill and dying in his quarters, leaving Lieutenant Coghlan as the only effective officer for the company.

During October, word apparently came back from the men still laboring at the Ajo del Carrizo lumber camp, that a band of hostile Apache Indians were lurking in their vicinity. Corporal Sabino Valdez and two privates from Company A, along with 30 California cavalrymen, were sent out to attempt capture of the Indians on October 31. They took with them the guide-spy and scout who served at Fort Bowie, named Merejildo Grijalva, to aid them in their efforts. On November 5, they attacked an Indian rancheria at Mescal Canyon, about 72 kilometers (45 miles) from the fort. They killed 17 Indians and wounded a number of others. A large quantity of mescal was destroyed, as well as the Indians' winter stores of provisions. The soldiers took four horses and one cow, some saddles, and skins the Indians were using for clothing and bedding. They returned to the fort on November 7.[38]

On November 9, in Santa Fe, a commission as first lieutenant was issued for Lieutenant Coghlan. He was to be promoted and transferred to another post. The paperwork, however, did not reach him at Fort Bowie until January 25, 1866. Coghlan could not be spared from Company A, however, for his departure would have left the company seriously short of officers. Coghlan also could not be promoted until he could find a mustering officer to carry out the official act and none was available in the area. The result was that he remained at Fort Bowie carrying out his duties as a second lieutenant until the company was on its way home. On August 8, 1866, at Fort Craig on the Rio Grande, Coghlan was finally mustered in as a first lieutenant and transferred to Company

I, although he did not join Company I until both companies were in Albuquerque being processed for discharge. After Company I was disbanded, Lieutenant Coghlan was retained in the service at his request and assigned to the Battalion of New Mexico Volunteers for service along the northern border of New Mexico.

Later in the month, on November 26, 20 of the New Mexico infantrymen, with 20 California cavalrymen, were sent out on an Indian scout to the Chiricahua Mountains north of the post, outfitted with 4 day's rations and 40 rounds of ammunition per man.[39] No results of this detail are recorded, probably because no contact was made. Many of these expeditions apparently failed to result in a direct confrontation but had harrassment value, keeping the Indians on the move and locked into a defensive posture.

Nine days after return of the scouting party, on December 9, Sergeants Mariano Sena and Melquiades Romero, with 18 men of Company A, accompanied 20 California cavalrymen under the command of Lieutenant Norton of the California volunteers, on an Indian scouting party in the Chiricahua Mountains again.[40] They didn't return until 2 days before Christmas, and covered 338 kilometers (210 miles) during their search. The duration and frequency of these scouts point to increased Indian activity in the area, however, again, no results of the search are recorded.

During their absence, on December 15, Captain James Mann, who had been recently promoted while serving with Company I at Fort Goodwin, arrived as Captain Quintana's replacement. Although only 28, Company A's new commander was very experienced in Western military operations.

The Indians were evidently still a problem, with reports probably coming into the fort, because on January 9, 1866, Captain Mann was ordered to take 35 of his men from Company A out on another Indian scout.[41] They were

20

rationed for 15 days and supplied with the necessary pack mules, camp, and garrison equipment. Fort Bowie post returns state that the scouting party found no Indians, discovering only several old rancherias which had been deserted from 3 to 9 months.

On February 1, 1866, Lieutenant Tapia died at Fort Bowie after having been ill for a year. He was not replaced and for the balance of the existence of Company A, it operated with only two officers.

On February 11, two noncommissioned officers and 12 men of the company were detailed to escort a wagon train, owned by Messrs Tully and Ochoa, as far as Agua Prieta at the Mexican border.[42] The train was bound for Fronteras, Mexico, 48 kilometers (30 miles) south of Agua Prieta, but the escort stopped at the border and waited there until the train returned and then escorted it back to Fort Bowie. The orders said, "The utmost vigilance will be displayed by this detachment on the route to prevent surprise or attack from Indians. The noncommissioned officers in charge will see that their men do not straggle on the march and when in camp to post the proper sentinels to insure the safety of all."

On February 15, one noncommissioned officer and 10 privates of Company A were detailed to finish work on a new road which was being constructed and on February 21, one noncommissioned officer and nine privates of the company were detailed to escort a wagon train, which had arrived with U.S. subsistence stores that day, on its trip back to Tucson.[43] The party left the next morning with orders to return as soon as possible with a six-mule team which would have been loaded with stores for Fort Bowie by the Department Quartermaster at Tucson.

Although James Mann had received a commission as captain, when he arrived at Fort Bowie to command Company A, he had not been mustered in officially. For a period of time he was assigned as acting captain but by March, 1866, when he still had been unable to find a mustering officer, he was required to act once again as a first lieutenant. He was not mustered in as a captain until June, 1866.

On March 17, one noncommissioned officer and nine privates of Company A were detailed to escort Mr. Tully, the trader, as far as Fort Cummings.[44] They were furnished with one pack mule and given 5 day's rations. On April 10, more men of Company A escorted a train to Tucson and again, on April 26, another trip was made to Tucson to pick up subsistence stores for Fort Bowie, and one noncommissioned officer and 13 privates from the company were sent to escort it.[45] This frequent escort duty, both east and west along the trail that made its way through Apache Pass, required the men to walk long distances through rugged terrain in all kinds of weather conditions. It, combined with the Indian scouts, construction duties, work at the post, and outpost duties, must have kept the men of Company A constantly busy.

Records show that on May 6, a detachment of Company A men, consisting of seven privates and one noncommissioned officer, was ordered to relieve a cavalry detail doing duty at the San Pedro River.[46] The men were apparently stationed at a point on the San Pedro between Fort Bowie and Tucson where crossings were made. The spot was evidently a 2-day trip away from Bowie, for the noncom in charge was told to issue 2-days' rations and forage from the stores to the relieved cavalrymen before they left to return to the fort.

Orders issued during the time Company A was stationed in Arizona show that in addition to their other duties, privates were also assigned jobs as teamsters, butchers, herders, carpenters, blacksmiths, masons, and hospital attendants.

On May 7, 1866, Captain W. Harvey Brown, with his Company E, Fourteenth U.S.

21

Infantry, arrived at Fort Bowie and assumed command. These Regular Army troops would replace the volunteers whose tour of duty was almost up. One of Captain Brown's first official acts was to issue Special Order No. 4, on May 10, just 2 days after his arrival, stating that due to the scarcity of wood at the post, none would be used except in officer's quarters, the first sergeant's quarters, for cooking and for laundry. He threatened that if any of the men were caught using wood illegally they would be confined to the guard house.

The men of Company A did not leave Fort Bowie immediately, however, but served at the post concurrently with the Regular Army soldiers for almost a month, giving rise to an amusing incident which was to cap their service at the fort. According to the memoirs of Sergeant John Spring, one of the Regular Army replacements, a drum major in his company, named Dewitt, was concerned that he might lose his job and rank once they were stationed at Bowie.[47] In order to prove his worth, and avoid demotion, he took in hand Company A's two buglers, Private Jesus Bustos and another man, and attempted to teach them the bugle calls. Captain Brown ordered Dewitt to hold his teaching sessions in a small canyon, out of earshot of the post, and Dewitt had the buglers practice for several days accompanied by two of the Regular Army drummer boys. Once he was satisfied with the progress of his students, Dewitt announced to Captain Brown that his "band" was prepared to undertake a creditable "retreat" at the close of the usual sunset dress parade. All the troops at the post, both the Regular Army men and the members of Company A, were very much interested in the matter and anxious to witness the performance.

One factor, however, had been overlooked. Spring stated the men of his company had brought with them a variety of stray dogs which they had picked up as pets at the Pima villages and in Tucson on their way to the post. In addition, the men of Company A were already the proud owners of a canine contingent which Spring described, "as remarkable for breed and color as for ugliness and utter worthlessness."

That evening, as the troops came to "parade rest," the musicians began their performance. As Spring describes it, "...as soon as the bugles started giving forth sounds that seemed to come from the subterranean caverns of the damned, all the dogs in the immediate vicinity, to the number of about 30, squatted on their haunches and broke forth in the most heart-rending howlings. The echo of their howls, coming back tenfold from the surrounding hills, combined with the accompaniment from the dogs taken up to as far a distance as the most remote canines could hear, made up a veritable pandemonium. Oh, it was grand!"

Spring reported that Captain Brown turned purple with fury and looked as though he might leap upon the drum major and strangle him while the entire ceremony turned into a shambles with the men laughing until their sides ached.

There were two immediate results of the aborted dress parade. First, the drum corps was disbanded with great speed and the drum major relegated to the ranks as a private. In the second place, on orders from the incensed Captain Brown, a great slaughter of all the dogs, except two valuable hunting dogs and a fine mastiff, was carried out by a detail of men selected for their marksmanship. Undoubtedly, the story of the Company A buglers would be told many times, long after they had departed from Fort Bowie.

In June, after completing 2 year's duty at Fort Bowie, Company A received orders to proceed to Fort Cummings and then on to Fort Craig on the Rio Grande, on their way north to be mustered out. The men were directed to kill all Indian men they might encounter or could find en route.[48]

On June 4, 1866, the company left Fort Bowie, arriving at Fort Cummings 5 days later after a 193 kilometers (120-mile) march. Lieutenant Coghlan, who had been acting assistant quartermaster at the post, remained behind for five days completing the paperwork necessary to turn over the public property. On June 12, after a short rest, the men left Cummings and traveled 97 kilometers (60 miles) to Fort Selden, which is 23 kilometers (14 miles) north of Las Cruces, arriving 2 days later.[49] After a 10-day stay they left the fort on June 24 and started northward up the Rio Grande toward Fort Craig, their next stop on the march north to Albuquerque. Left behind was Private Jose Martin, of Santa Fe, who was apparently too ill to continue on with the company. He died at Fort Selden on July 6, of causes not listed.

Spirits must have been high among the rest of the men who had originally enlisted in Santa Fe and northern New Mexico, for they were finally headed home after an absence of 2½ years. But there was to be disappointment. During their march to Fort Craig, a message arrived from Brevet Major Burkett of the California volunteers, directing their return south to Fort Cummings to assist in a planned Indian scout in the direction of Pinos Altos, north of present-day Silver City. Burkett had been ordered, by Carleton's Santa Fe headquarters, to use all troops available to him to make a concentrated effort to find and kill, in the Pinos Altos area, Indians who reportedly had committed some murders.[50]

Probably disheartened at this turn of events, the men of Company A retraced their route back to Fort Cummings. On June 27, outfitted with 25 days' rations, and under the command of Major Burkett, they left Cummings at 10 o'clock at night and marched 29

kilometers (18 miles) westward to Camp Mimbres, New Mexico. Two days later they traveled another 9.6 kilometers (6 miles) to Hot Springs, where a camp site was set up.[51] They participated in the Indian campaign for slightly more than a month. Records do not show the activities of the bulk of Company A but Special Order No. 45, dated July 9, shows that Corporal Miguel Gonzales and five privates were detailed to go to the Rio Mimbres Crossing and remain there until further orders, as a guard unit for protection of the settlers and ranchmen of that place and that they were rationed until the end of the month.[52] Also, on July 28, Sergeant Jose Pena and eight privates were detailed to Hot Springs as protection to families there. They were issued rations to last until August 3.[53] The main purpose of the campaign, however, had been to punish the Apaches in the "Gila and Mimbres River Mountains" and it can be assumed the bulk of Company A was involved in the process of trying to find and kill Indians.

By August 4, Company A's role in the Indian scout was completed and they were relieved of duty and told to proceed, via Fort Selden, to Albuquerque, there to await further orders.[54] The men marched to Albuquerque without further incident. On August 31, 1866, 11 men of Company A were transferred to a new organization called Battalion of New Mexico Volunteers. The remainder were discharged on September 26, in Albuquerque, and Company A, First New Mexico Volunteers, was deactivated.

The new battalion, composed of men from both the First New Mexico Infantry and the First New Mexico Cavalry Volunteers who still had a good portion of their enlistments left to serve, was organized into four companies of 98 men each, two of infantry and two of cavalry. The officers were chosen by General Carleton from among those who desired to remain in the

23

service. The battalion, under the command of Kit Carson, was sent to Fort Garland, Colorado, for service along the northern frontier of New Mexico where difficulties with the Ute Indians were being encountered.[55]

Company A had been an active organization for three years. Most of its service had been in Arizona where the hazards and hardships had been compounded by isolation, understaffing, and lack of decent facilities and weapons. Saddled with an enormous workload and deficient in manpower, the men of Company A were required to expend great effort both in escorting supply trains and travelers and in frequent Indian searches in the hostile, rugged Chiricahua Mountains which rise to 2,987 meters (9,796 feet). The soldiers' presence kept the dangerous pass open.

Under these extreme conditions, a few men deserted, others endured, and some became ill. Of the 10 men who deserted during the time in Arizona, seven had been born in old Mexico, and four had never been mustered in and therefore probably were not being paid. Sickness was always a problem at the fort. Records show that during the summer of 1865, Sergeant Dolores Anaya was discharged at Bowie, suffering from rheumatism, at about the time Private Lucero died there. It even seems reasonable to assume that Private Martin, who died on the way home, probably was already ill before he left the fort. Captain Quintana was sent away because of poor health, but the most poignant story is that of Lieutenant Juan Climaca Tapia, who was 31 years old when he first arrived at Fort Bowie. Tapia was the oldest of three children born to a poor family in Santa Fe. During his youth he was taken under the wing of a prominent and wealthy Santa Fe man, Donaciano Vigil, a long-time friend of the family. Vigil, in a sworn statement made to assist Tapia's mother in obtaining a pension from the government, said, "Juan C. Tapia, before entering said service (military), was from child-

hood under my custody as a clerk and otherwise, up to the date of becoming of age; that I schooled and educated him in great part."[56]

Tapia, a conscientious son, supported his parents after his father, an elderly man, became ill and unable to work. From 1854 to 1857 he held the post of Territorial Librarian in Santa Fe.[57] This job had been established a few years earlier in an attempt to safeguard official books and documents, but little money was available for financing its operation. The salary was only $100 a year, and while several small rooms were set aside for the books, the librarian was required to supply the wood necessary to heat the rooms himself. Tapia, at 21, was probably glad to take a job that paid a cash salary, but after he quit the post remained open for several years because no other literate applicant wanted it. Later, before his enlistment in the military in late 1863, Juan worked in the Surgeon General's office in Santa Fe. Even while he was stationed at Fort Bowie, Juan Tapia sent his parents money to assure their well-being.

Shortly after arrival at Fort Bowie with Company A, he was sent out on an Indian scout, and thereafter, appeared to be almost constantly on field duty for the next 6 months since he was the only Company A officer available to go. The rigors of the long marches, limited diet, bad water taken wherever it could be found in arid country, sleeping on the ground, exposure to inclement weather, all apparently took their toll on Tapia's health. When ordered, in January, 1865, to set up the lumber camp, he apparently was already ill; nevertheless, he marched his men there and set to work. By early February, word had already been sent back to Fort Bowie that Tapia was too sick with hepatitis to continue on duty and he was relieved and returned to the post. Throughout March and April he lay ill in his quarters, too sick to perform any duties. By May his condition had improved enough for him to go back on duty but by July he was once again bedridden. After more months of illness, he wrote a letter on November 22, tending his resignation as an officer, saying, "I have been in very ill health for the past 3½ months quite unfit for duty and feel little probability of recovery at this station." Tapia, desperately ill, sensed that his chances for improvement under the primitive conditions in existence at the fort were slim so he also requested a furlough "for such period as you see fit pending action on this request." Tapia's request was not to be acted upon and after his death, bitterness was expressed by several of the people who assisted his mother in applying for a pension. They stated that Juan Tapia had been in robust good health his entire life until he was sent to Arizona, and Donaciano Vigil stated that Tapia had died of disease "contracted while in the military service of the United States, and in the line of his duty, and occasioned from exposure in camp, and the inferiority of quarters wherein he was stationed, said to have been mere hovels cut into the earth on a side hill and roofed over.."

Enclosed with Tapia's resignation letter was a letter from the Post Surgeon which said:

> I have examined this officer carefully and find he is suffering from Chronic Hepatitis with doubtless complications of an organic nature. He has been under my charge on Sick Report unfit for duty since Aug. 15, 1865. He is totally unfit for duty and in my opinion his complete recovery is very doubtful and date uncertain. I am furthermore of the opinion that an immediate change of locality is absolutely necessary and the only chance which may lead to an improvement of his condition.

For some reason, possibly indifference or bureaucratic slowness, Tapia's request to leave the fort was futile. For the next 2½ months he lay, slowly dying, in his quarters. On January 8, the army discharged Tapia, but he, at the lonely outpost, was unaware of it. Almost providentially, on January 24, 1866, the Reverend John Baptist Salpointe, a Catholic priest, arrived at Fort Bowie. Salpointe, a protege of Bishop Lamy, had come from Tapia's home town of Santa Fe and was on his way, with other missionaries, to give spiritual aid to Catholics of the Arizona Territory. Salpointe's account of the trip stated he was allowed to use the post hospital tent to say Mass for the soldiers and that he was "able to assist a dying man, Captain (sic) Tapia from Santa Fe, and give him the last sacraments of the Church."[58] On the first day of February, 1866, Juan Tapia died, still at Fort Bowie. He had been ill there for 1 year before his death, yet was never allowed to return to his home and family in Santa Fe.

A list of Tapia's personal effects, made by the military, showed that among his possessions were a bear skin, $500 in United States currency, two pistols, and a carbine. Tapia's father had died the year before and the money was sent to his mother. It helped sustain her for several years but she then became destitute and dependent on charity.

Although the records do not show that Company A was involved in any particularly dramatic battles against large groups of Apaches during its tour of duty as part of the Apache Expedition, an examination of the very incomplete records does show its many activities. When considered, in light of conditions in effect at the time and the limited manpower available, they do, however, represent a formidable accomplishment. General Carleton himself said that Apache Pass, Arizona, was by far the most dangerous point on the southern route to California and Company A played its part in keeping the way open for safe travel.

25

ADDENDUM

I n investigating the many sources necessary to create the history of Company A, a number of facts, not essential to the story, were uncovered. Since some of this information might prove to be of interest to historical researchers and scholars, or to descendants of some of the Company A personnel who are investigating family histories, it is being included here along with the compilation of some data.

General Information on Company A Personnel

Place of Birth:
Mexico 25
Arizona 3
Texas 1
New Mexico 42
Ohio 1
Unknown 54

Average Height:
5'3" to 5'6"
Average Age:
Born between 1835 and 1845

Deserted: 32 men

Died: 6 men

Disabled: 2 men

Ethnic Make-up of Company: 126 total
      4 Anglo
    122 Spanish (including one Navajo with Spanish name)

	Total	Anglo	Spanish
Officers	5	3	2
1st Sgt.	1	1	0
Sgt.	8	0	8
Cpl.	16	0	16
Pvt.	119	0	119

NOTE: Figures above reflect the fact some enlisted men held several ranks.

DIED

Name	Date	Location	Cause
Pvt. Vivian Lucero	July 24, 1865	Ft. Bowie, A.T.	Unknown
Pvt. Jose Martin	July 5, 1865	Ft. Selden, N.M.	Unknown
Pvt. Jose Maria Romero	Dec. 20, 1863	Ft. Marcy, N.M.	Unknown
Pvt. Mauricio Silva	May 22, 1864	Belen, N.M.	Shot by guard
1st Lt. Juan Climaca Tapia	Feb. 1, 1866	Ft. Bowie, A.T.	Chronic hepatitis
Pvt. Olayio Tarin	April 29, 1864	Ft. Union, N.M.	Shot at Loma Parda

DISABLED

	Name	Date	Location	Cause
28	Sgt. Dolores Anaya	June 26, 1865	Ft. Bowie, A.T.	Rheumatism
	Pvt. Miguel Tapia	June 26, 1865	Ft. Union, N.M.	Syphilis

DESERTED

Thirty-two men, out of a total of 126, deserted from Company A, which is a 25% desertion rate. This rate must be considered very reasonable when compared to the 33% desertion rate attributed to the Regular Army troops who had enlisted between 1867 and 1891. (See p. 143.) Don Rickey, Jr.'s book, *Forty Miles a Day on Beans and Hay*. It should also be remembered that the Regular Army men spoke English but the volunteers were Spanish-speakers in an organization whose rules and regulations were couched in a language they did not understand. It is also interesting to note that only 10 men deserted during the 2-year period while the company was stationed in Arizona, carrying out its most hazardous duty.

Pvt. Jose Ignacio Abeitia   Jan. 16, 1864   Ft. Union, N.M.
  (Apprehended March 2, '64, confined till June, '64, released, served honorably till discharge)
Pvt. Miguel Abeitia   Apr. 20, 1864   Ft. Union, N.M.
Pvt. Jesus Aldiya   Oct. 3, 1865   Ft. Bowie, A.T.
Pvt. Juan Jose Apodaca   Dec. 6, 1863   Ft. Union, N.M.
Pvt. Juan Cota   Aug. 7, 1865   Ft. Bowie, A.T. (Never mustered)
Pvt. Nasario Crespin   Dec. 6, 1863   Ft. Union, N.M.
  (Caught Feb. 29, '64, confined, drummed out of service, Sept. 8, '64 at Ft. Craig)
Pvt. Victorino Dominguez   Feb. 8, 1864   Ft. Union, N.M.
  (Apprehended Apr. 15, '64, sentenced to death, released May 10, '65, served honorably till discharge)

Pvt. Jose Maria Eldaco	Aug. 7, 1865	Ft. Bowie, A. T.
Pvt. Hilario Gallegos	Aug. 11, 1864	Ft. Bowie, A. T.
Pvt. Nestor Gallegos	Dec. 25, 1863	Ft. Union, N.M.
Pvt. Eloy Gonzales	June 25, 1866	Ft. Selden, N.M.
Pvt. Jose Miguel Griego	Dec. 2, 1863	Ft. Union, N.M.

(Apprehended on Dec. 19, '64, confined, drummed out of service on July 17, 1864)

Pvt. Jose Maria Gutierres	May 16, 1864	Carnuel, N.M.
Pvt. Cristobal Isco	May 7, 1866	Tucson, A.T.
Cpl. Jose Antonio Leiba	May 14, 1864	Las Cruces, N.M.

(Rejoined company, May 26, '65, served honorably until transferred to Company H)

Pvt. Salvador Lobato	Dec. 12, 1863	Ft. Union, N.M.
Pvt. Juan Nepomoseno Lucero #1	Nov. 28, 1863	Enroute to Ft. Union, N.M.

(Apprehended on Jan. 30, '64, confined, drummed out of service, Sept. 8, '64)

Pvt. Juan Nepomoseno Lucero #2	Dec. 25, 1863	Ft. Union, N.M.
Pvt. Juan Martin	Dec. 25, 1863	Ft. Union, N.M.
Pvt. Luis Montez	June 25, 1866	Unknown
Pvt. George Rebero	Feb. 15, 1866	Agua Prieta, Mexico
Pvt. Juan Salazar	Dec. 25, 1863	Ft. Union, N.M.
Pvt. Lucas Salazar	Aug. 7, 1865	Ft. Bowie, A.T. (Never mustered)
Pvt. Mauricio Silva	Dec. 12, 1863	Ft. Union, N.M.

(Caught, killed in escape attempt, May 22, '64 at Belen, N.M.)

Pvt. Francisco Sisneros	Dec. 25, 1863	Ft. Union, N.M.
Sgt. Miguel Tapia	Jan. 16, 1864	Ft. Union, N.M.

(Apprehended on Feb. 23, '64, discharged on June 26, '65 for disability, as a private)

Pvt. Juan Telles	Mar. 27, 1865	Tubac, A.T.
Pvt. Jose Ramon Trujillo	Apr. 4, 1864	Ft. Union, N.M.
Pvt. Juan de Jesus Trujillo	Apr. 4, 1864	Ft. Union, N.M.
Pvt. Francisco Pena Vasques	Apr. 8, 1864	Ft. Union, N.M.
Pvt. Ignacio Villa	Oct. 24, 1864	Ft. Bowie, A.T. (Never mustered)
Pvt. Francisco Zinogui	Oct. 24, 1864	Ft. Bowie, A.T. (Never mustered)

All information listed was gleaned from Individual Service Records, Source #10 (See footnotes).

PRIOR MILITARY SERVICE

Records are extremely poor in reference to prior military service, particularly for the enlisted men of low rank. Listed below is what information is known regarding earlier service, but it is highly likely that some other members of the company had seen military duty of some sort before enlisting in Company A.

Sgt. Jose Maria Castillo: 2nd Infantry, New Mexico Volunteers, 1862.
1st Sgt. Christian Noedell: Company E, 8th U.S. Infantry, July 1855 to July 1860.

Sgt. Mariano Sena: 1st New Mexico Militia, 1862.

Sgt. Miguel Tapia: 1st New Mexico Militia, 1861–1862.

Capt. Nicolas Quintana: 2nd Lt., Company C, 1st New Mexico Infantry Volunteers (Old), 1861–1862. Participated at Battle of Valverde.

Capt. James Mann: Served 6 years in Company F, 5th U.S. Infantry, 1857–1863. Participated in: 1) Utah Expedition against Mormons under General Albert S. Johnston, 2) Navajo Expedition under General Edward Canby, 3) Battle of Valverde and all other skirmishes against Texas which took place in New Mexico during 1862.

NOTE: Above information from Individual Service Records and C. Noedell's Pension Records.

EQUIPMENT

Listed below are the items officially requisitioned for Companies A and I prior to their departure from Fort Union for Arizona. The requisition was in accordance with the requirements of the Department of New Mexico. The Volunteers were apparently given less clothing than Regular Army soldiers who, for example, were normally supplied with four pairs of pants. Records show, in some cases, the only possessions some Volunteers had, at the time of their death, was the clothing they were buried in.

Each man was to be supplied with:

1 hat—trimmed	1 pr. pants
1 cap	1 coat
2 shirts	1 great coat
2 pr. drawers	1 blanket
2 pr. socks	1 knapsack & haversack & canteen
1 pr. new bootees	

Company property would include:

6 camp kettles	2 hatchets
10 mess pans or frying pans	4 spades
4 axes	4 pick axes

For messing purposes the men were each to have his own:

tin cup	knife, fork, spoon
tin plate	(sheath knife preferable)

For toilet purposes each man would have:

1 coarse comb	1 towel and a piece of soap

The Company was to be supplied with 20,000 rounds of ammunition. (Info from Source #10.)

30

Courtesy Dr. Francis A. Lord
Lord Americana & Research, Inc.
1521 Redwood Drive
W. Columbia, S.C.

Shoes or "bootees." These shoes are of heavy leather, with the rough side to the outside.
No grommets in lace holes. Laces of rawhide. Squared toe, heavy leather sole and heel.

COMPANY A
ROSTER

L isted below is a roster of the men in Company A. Maximum authorized strength for a New Mexico Volunteer Infantry Company was: 1 Captain, 1 First Lieutenant, 1 Second Lieutenant, 1 First Sergeant, 4 Sergeants, 8 Corporals, 2 Musicians, 1 Wagoner, and from 64 to 82 Privates. Companies, however, were seldom up to full strength.[59]

In the list below, a soldier's name can be listed more than once if he was promoted, i.e., once as a private and again as a corporal, for the roster shows the names of those who served at each rank during the life of the company. All names were obtained from official records, however, some inaccuracies or misspellings are probable since most paper work was done by English-speaking men who could misinterpret spoken Spanish in which, for example, the letter "V" often sounds like a "B".[60]

CAPTAIN

QUINTANA, Nicolas   MANN, James

1ST LIEUTENANT

LAUER, Henry W.   TAPIA, Juan Climaca

2ND LIEUTENANT

TAPIA, Juan Climaca   COGHLAN, Thomas

1ST SERGEANT

NOEDELL, Christian

SERGEANT

ANAYA, Dolores   ROMERO, Melquiades
CASTILLO, Jose Maria   SENA, Mariano
MARTINEZ, Candelario   TAPIA, Miguel
PENA, Jose Ramos   VALDEZ, Sabino

CORPORAL

ARANDA, Diego Antonio   LEIBA, Jose Antonio
BARRERES, Miguel   MONTOYA, Benicio
CASTILLO, Jose Maria   ORTIZ, Agapito
CONTRERAS, Jesus   PENA, Jose Ramos
CRISPIN, Jesus Maria   ROIBAL, Ignacio
GALLEGOS, Santiago   ROMERO, Melquiades
GONZALES, Miguel   SILVA, Jose S.
HERRERA, Jesus De   VALDEZ, Sabino

33

PRIVATE

ABEITIA, Jose Ignacio
ABEITIA, Miguel
ACUNIE, Jesus
ALBAREZ, Anselmo
ALDIYA, Jesus
APODACA, Juan Jose
ARANDA, Diego Antonio
ARMIJO, Neponaceno

BALDONADO, Alexandro
BARRERAS, Estevan
BARRERES, Miguel
BLEA, Anado
BURNELLA, Crecencio
BUSTOS, Jesus

CARDENES, Querino
CASTILLO, Jose Marìa
CHAVES, Rafael
CHAVEZ, Francisco
CONTRERAS, Jesus
COTA, Juan
CRESPIN, Nasario
CRISPIN, Jesus Maria
CRUZ, Jose Santa

DIAS, Emilio
DOMINGUEZ, Victorino
DUARTE, Francisco
DURAN, Doroteo

ELDACO, Jose Maria

FIMBRES, Jose

GABALDON, Juan
GALLEGOS, Canuto
GALLEGOS, Hilario
GALLEGOS, Nestor
GALLEGOS, Santiago
GONZALES, Eloy
GONZALES, Miguel
GONZALES, Santiago

GRIEGO, Aniceto
GRIEGO, Jose Miguel
GRIEGO, Juan Francisco
GUTIERRES, Francisco
GUTIERRES, Jose Maria

HERNANDEZ, Jesus
HERRERA, Jesus De
HERRERA, Miguel Antonio

ISCO, Cristobal

LEAL, Jose Dolores
LEIBA, Jose Antonio
LICON, Pedro
LOBATO, Salvador
LOPEZ, Miguel
LUCERO, Cornelio
LUCERO, Juan Nepomoseno #1
LUCERO, Juan Nepomoseno #2
LUCERO, Vivian

MADRID, Feliz
MARQUIS, Antonio
MARTIN, Candelario
MARTIN, Desiderio
MARTIN, Felipe
MARTIN, Jose
MARTIN, Juan
MARTIN, Julian
MARTIN, Librado
MARTIN, Manuel Antonio
MARTIN, Melquiades
MARTIN, Ramon
MENDOZA, Crecencio
MENDOZA, Jose
MESTAS, Mauricio
MOLLA, Santiago
MONTEZ, Luis
MONTOYA, Benicio
MONTOYA, Juan
MONTOYA, Rafael
MUNOZ, Encarnacion

NAVARRO, Seledonio

OCHOA, Jesus
ORTEGA, Alejo
ORTIZ, Agapito
ORTIZ, Francisco
ORTIZ, Juan

PACHECO, Eustaquio
PADILLA, Antonio
PADILLA, Casimiro
PENA, Jose Ramos
PEREA, Domingo

REBERO, George
RENDON, Jose
RODRIGUEZ, Juan
ROIBAL, Ignacio
ROMERO, Carmel
ROMERO, Jose Maria
ROMERO, Melquiades
ROMERO, Pimenio

SALAZAR, Francisco
SALAZAR, Juan
SALAZAR, Lucas
SALAZAR, Trinidad
SANCHES, Jose
SANDOBAL, Epitacio
SENA, Jesus Maria
SENA, Mariano
SILVA, Jose S.
SILVA, Mauricio
SISNEROS, Francisco

TAFOYA, Jose Antonio
TAPIA, Miguel
TARIN, Olayio
TRUJILLO, Jose
TRUJILLO, Jose Ramon
TRUJILLO, Juan de Jesus

VALDEZ, Sabino
VASQUES, Francisco Pena
VELASQUEZ, Miguel
VILLA, Ignacio

ZINOGUI, Francisco

35

MUSICIAN

BUSTOS, Jesus   TELLES, Juan

LAUNDRESS

FLORES, Juana   MESTES, Predencia

FOOTNOTES

NOTE: To avoid repetitive listings of long-titled National Archives microfilmed sources, each of these sources has been assigned a reference number and will be identified here at the beginning of the footnotes. Other sources are footnoted in the conventional manner.

Source #1—Record Group 94, Records of the Adjutant General, "Post Returns of Fort Cummings, N.M., 1863–1873."

Source #2—Record Group 98, "Post Orders, Fort Cummings, N.M., 1863–1873."

Source #3—Record Group 94, Returns from U.S. Military Post, Fort McRae, N.M., June 1863–Oct. 1876, Microcopy 617, Roll 710.

Source #4—Record Group 393, Records of U.S. Army Continental Command, 1821–1920, Fort Selden, N.M., "Letters Sent," Vol. 7A-1866, pp. 1–49.

Source #5—Record Group 393, Records of U.S. Army Continental Command, 1821–1920, Fort Selden, N.M., "General and Special Orders," Vols. 23A and 23B.

Source #6—Record Group 94, Returns from U.S. Military Post, 1800–1916, Fort Selden, N.M., May 1865–Dec. 1871, Microcopy 617, Roll 1145.

Source #7—Record Group 94, Post Returns of U.S. Military Posts, 1800–1916, Fort Bowie, A.T.

Source #8—Record Group 94, Records of the Adjutant Generals Office, 1783–1917, Regimental Record Book, Civil War, 1st Reg., N.M. Infantry, "Letters Sent and Received and Orders, 1861–1866."

Source #9—Record Group 393, Records of U.S. Army Continental Command, 1821–1920, Fort Union, N.M.

Source #10—Record Group 94, Compiled Service Records of Volunteer Union Soldiers who served in Organizations from the Territory of New Mexico, Microcopy 427.

Source #11—Record Group 94, Records of the Adjutant Generals Office, "Post Returns from U.S. Military Post, 1800–1916," Fort Goodwin, A.T., Microcopy 617.

Source #12—Record Group 94, Records of the Adjutant General Office, Misc. File 160.

1. Individual Muster Roll of Candelario Martinez, Source #10. *NOTE:* Hereafter, information gleaned from Individual Muster Rolls will *not* be footnoted. Facts can be verified by examination of records in Source #10, looking under individual soldier's name.

2. Arrott Collection, Highlands University, Las Vegas, New Mexico.

3. Company Muster Roll, December 31, 1863, Source #10.

4. S.O. 23, Headquarters, Dept. of New Mexico, Santa Fe, June 25, 1864, Arrott Collection.

5. S.O. 30, Hqtrs., Dept. of N.M., September 21, 1864, Arrott Collection. Also see *Santa Fe New Mexican*, Sept. 30, 1864, for story on deserters.

6. S.O. 13, Dept. of N.M., Source #8.

7. Company Muster Roll, May, 1864, Source #10 and S.O. 85, Hqtrs., Fort Union, May 6, 1864, Source #8.

8. S.O. 1, Hqtrs., Dept. of Apache Expedition, Las Cruces, N.M., June 4, 1864, Source #8.

9. S.O. 3, Hqtrs., 4th District, Apache Expedition, Camp at Cienaga, June 16, 1864, Source #8.

10. Company Returns, June, 1864, Source #10.

11. *Fort Bowie,* U.S. Dept. of the Interior, National Park Service, G.P.O., 1975

12. Richard Y. Murray, "The History of Fort Bowie," unpublished Master of Arts thesis, University of Arizona, 1951, p. 105.

13. Post Returns, 1864, Fort Bowie National Historic Site, Arizona.

14. *Official Report, War of the Rebellion,* Series 1, Vol. 41, Book 2, (Washington, D.C.:G.P.O., 1897), pp. 277–278.

15. Post Returns, 1864, Fort Bowie National Historic Site, Arizona.

16. *Official Report, War of the Rebellion,* Series 1, Vol. 50, Book 2, pp. 1134–1135.

17. Company Returns, July, 1864, Source #10.

18. G.O. 12, Hqtrs., Dept. of N.M., Santa Fe, May 1, 1864, Arrott Collection.

19. Fort Bowie Post Returns, Sept. and Dec., 1864 and Jan. 1865, Source #7.

20. Lt. Col. C. E. Bennett to Lt. E. W. Wood, Las Cruces, N.M., Dec. 19, 1864, Source #8.

21. Col. F. P. Abreu to Maj. B. C. Cutler, June 27, 1865. Arrott Collection.

22. S.O. 1, Hqtrs., Ft. Bowie, A.T., Jan. 15, 1865, Source #8.

23. Ibid.

24. Lt. Col. C. E. Bennett to Col. J. C. McFerran, Feb. 11, 1865, *Official Report, War of the Rebellion*, Series 1, Vol. 50, Book 2, pp. 1134–1135.

25. S.O. 1, Hqtrs., Ft. Bowie, A.T., Jan. 15, 1865, Source #8.

26. S.O. 3, Hqtrs., Ft. Bowie, A.T., Feb. 6, 1865, Source #8.

27. Fort Bowie Post Returns, Feb. 1865, Source #7 and S.O. 5, Hqtrs., Ft. Bowie, Feb. 15, 1865, Source #8.

28. S.O. 8, Hqtrs., Ft. Bowie, A.T., March 8, 1865, Source #8 and S.O. 7, Hqtrs., Ft. Bowie, March 5, 1865, Source #8.

29. Lt. Col. C. E. Bennett to Col. R. C. Drum, March 19, 1865, *The War of the Rebellion*, Series 1, Vol. 50, Book 2, pp. 1164–1165.

30. S.O. 10, Hqtrs., Ft. Bowie, A.T., March 21, 1865, Source #8.

31. S.O. 17, Hqtrs., Ft. Bowie, A.T., April 25, 1865, Source #8.

32. Fort Bowie Succession of Command, 1865–1866, Fort Bowie Historical Site Records, Ariz.

33. Lt. Col. C. E. Bennett to Capt. John Green, July 21, 1865, *Official Records, War of the Rebellion*, Series 1, Volume 50, Book 1, pp. 421–423.

34. S.O. 27, Hqtrs., Ft. Bowie, A.T., July 4, 1865, Source #8 and Capt. N. Quintana to Capt. C. De-Forrest, Ft. Craig, N.M., May 28, 1864, Source #8.

35. S.O. 29, Hqtrs., Ft. Bowie, A.T., July 11, 1865, Source #8.

36. S.O. 37, Hqtrs., Ft. Bowie, A.T., Aug. 31, 1865, Source #8.

37. G.O. 10, Hqtrs., Ft. Bowie, A.T., July 25, 1865, Source #8.

38. "Record of Events at Ft. Bowie During Nov., 1865," Ft. Bowie National Historic Site, Ariz., S.O. 55, Hqtrs., Ft. Bowie, Oct. 31, 1865, Source #8, and Company Muster Roll, Nov.–Dec., 1865, Source #10.

39. S.O. 67, Hqtrs., Ft. Bowie, A.T., Nov. 26, 1865, Source #8.

40. Company Returns, Nov.–Dec., 1865, Source #10.

41. S.O. 4, Hqtrs., Ft. Bowie, A.T., Jan. 9, 1866, Sources #7 and 8.

42. S.O. 17, Hqtrs., Ft. Bowie, A.T., Feb. 11, 1866, Source #8.

43. S.O. 19, Feb. 15, 1866 and S.O. 21, Feb. 21, 1866, both Hqtrs., Ft. Bowie, A.T., Source #8.

44. S.O. 36, Hqtrs., Ft. Bowie, A.T., March 17, 1866, Source #8.

45. S.O. 42, April 10, 1866 and S.O. 46, April 26, 1866, both Hqtrs., Ft. Bowie, A.T., Source #8.

46. S.O. 1, Hqtrs., Ft. Bowie, A.T., May 6, 1866, Source #8.

47. John Spring, *John Spring's Arizona*, ed. A. M. Gustafson (Tucson: The University of Arizona Press, 1966), pp. 49–50.

48. S.O. 17, Hqtrs., Dist. of N.M., Santa Fe, June 7, 1866, Arrott Collection.

49. Company Muster Roll, May–June 1866, Source #10.

50. Maj. C. DeForrest to Maj. G. A. Burkett, Santa Fe, N.M., June 14, 1866, Arrott Collection.

51. Company Muster Roll, May–June 1866, Source #10.

52. S.O. 45, Hqtrs., Ft. Cummings, N.M., July 9, 1866, Source #8.

53. S.O. 49, Hqtrs., Ft. Cummings, N.M., July 28, 1866, Source #2.

54. S.O. 22, Hqtrs., Dist. of N.M., Santa Fe, Aug. 4, 1866, Source #8.

55. General Field Order 4, Hqtrs., Dept. of Missouri, Santa Fe, N.M., July 21, 1866, Arrott Collection.

56. Deposition of Donaciano Vigil, Feb. 24, 1870, Santa Fe, N.M., Juan C. Tapia Military Pension Records, National Archives, Washington, D.C.

57. Arie Poldervaart, "The New Mexico Law Library—A History," *New Mexico Historical Review*, Vol. 21, No. 1, Jan., 1946, p. 48.

58. Most Reverend J. B. Salpointe, *Soldiers of the Cross* (Albuquerque: Calvin Horn, Publisher, Inc., 1967), p. 247.

59. Proclamation by Governor Henry Connelly, Santa Fe, Territory of New Mexico, Sept. 21, 1863, Source #12.

60. All names were obtained from Individual Muster Rolls, Source #10.

"I am convinced that the best troops that could be used in war with them (Indians) would be Mexicans as they are more energetic and untiring in pursuit, enduring a larger amount of physical fatigue and, when well-officered, their courage is unquestionable."

Brevet Brigadier General Christopher "Kit" Carson
to Brigadier General James Carleton, October, 1866

COMPANY I

1st INFANTRY NEW MEXICO VOLUNTEERS

Company I was conceived and born in Taos, a northern New Mexico town originally settled by the Spanish in 1617. Situated near the ancient Tewa Indian pueblo of the same name, Taos nestles in the pine-and-aspen-covered Sangre de Cristo Mountains 87 kilometers (54 miles) northeast of Santa Fe and only 72 kilometers (45 miles) south of the Colorado border.

The residents of Taos were a hardy breed in 1863, when recruiting for the company began. Most made their living raising stock or farming at the 2,135 meter (7,000-foot) altitude which contributed to a rather short growing season and frequent heavy winter snowstorms. However, fertile mountain soil and abundance of moisture allowed production of many foodstuffs by the diligent farmer.

The father of Company I was Captain Smith H. Simpson, a well-known local personality who had settled permanently at Taos in 1860. Simpson raised the company himself, recruiting in the Taos area from October, 1863, through January, 1864, and commanded it throughout its existence until it was disbanded in September, 1866.

Simpson was an adventurous and self-reliant man, born in New York City on May 8,

Smith H. Simpson, 1860
Courtesy of Kit Carson Museum
Taos, New Mexico

43

1833.[1] He was the grandson of a Revolutionary War soldier who reputedly was with Washington the night he made his famous Delaware River crossing.[2] Simpson, orphaned at 16 when both his parents died of cholera, set out to make his own living, working first in Pennsylvania and later in New Orleans as a clerk. Later, while in St. Joseph, Missouri, he obtained a position as second clerk with the chief quartermaster for New Mexico and traveled to Santa Fe in September, 1853. For the next 6 years he traveled widely, serving for 6 months as a commissary sergeant in the Ute War of 1855, running a government express over a large part of the West, and even journeying to Mexico City, New Orleans, and New York before he finally returned to New Mexico and settled down in Taos to farm and raise stock. In addition to these agricultural pursuits, Simpson acted, in 1859–1860, as Kit Carson's confidential clerk and secretary while Carson served as Indian agent in Taos.[3] In essence, Carson, an outdoorsman, handled all the "field" work while Simpson ran the agent's headquarters, making out reports, handling correspondence, and acting in a capacity that actually exceeded his title as clerk.

When the Civil War broke out, Carson and Simpson, both strong Union sympathizers, fastened the American flag to a pole and raised it over the Plaza in Taos. To insure against its being torn down by Confederate loyalists among the approximately 50 Anglo-Americans then living in Taos, both men took turns guarding the flag day and night during the critical period.[4] As a result of their actions, Taos today boasts the distinction of being the first place in the United States, by tradition, to fly Old Glory day and night.

When Governor Henry Connelly of New Mexico authorized reactivation of the First New Mexico Infantry Volunteers in September, 1863, Simpson decided to become a part of the organization. On October 28, he was granted tentative commission as a captain in the regiment. He would not be officially mustered-in until he had successfully raised enough men to fill a company. Simpson immediately began recruiting efforts in the Taos area, where he had a wide circle of acquaintances.

Most of the men recruited as privates were Spanish-speaking natives of Taos and surrounding small towns and villages. In the original organization, seven of the corporals were Hispanic and the eighth was a native of Germany. The four sergeants were evenly divided, two whose primary language was Spanish and two who were English-speakers. The first sergeant and all the company officers were Anglos but obviously were, or soon became, relatively competent in Spanish during the time they served with the men. First Sergeant David McAllister stated at a later date, that there were only two men in the company, beside himself, who could speak English.[5]

While Simpson was able to sign up many men to serve in the enlisted ranks, he was in dire need of several proficient not only in the English language but with some prior military experience to serve as his first and second lieutenants. By January, 1864, when it became apparent his recruiting efforts had been successful enough to insure the company would become a reality, he somehow managed to have First Lieutenant James Mann transferred from the then-existing Company G of the New Mexico Volunteers into the emerging Company I. The transfer had to be a coup for Simpson since the 27-year-old Mann was a very experienced soldier, having served for 6 years in the Regular Army as a noncommissioned infantryman and having fought, under General Canby, at the Battle of Valverde against the Texans in 1862. Mann was transferred to Company I on January 20, 1864, and now Simpson needed a second lieutenant.

During the winter, as Simpson recruited men in the Taos area, they were sent, in small groups, south to Fort Marcy in Santa Fe to be given physical examinations and outfitted. After they were processed they apparently were then sent on to Fort Union, once again in small groups, to await arrival of the balance of the company. By February 23, 1864, enough men had joined for the company to be officially enrolled by authority of Special Order 5, Headquarters, Department of New Mexico in Santa Fe.[6] This same order supplied Captain Simpson with his second lieutenant. Obviously affirming some earlier, unofficial arrangements, the order stated, "Sergeant Edward E. Ayer, of Company 'E' 1st Cavalry, California Volunteers, having been commissioned as a 2nd Lieutenant of Company 'I' of the 1st Regiment, New Mexico Volunteers, is hereby honorably discharged from the service of the United States as a Sergeant … that he may accept promotion …" Company I was now officially on duty, complete with three officers, and was instructed to "without delay proceed from Fort Marcy and take post at Fort Union." The men from Taos had no inkling that within 2 months they would be ordered, as one of two New Mexico volunteer companies, to march to Arizona and there campaign against the Apaches.

Company I left Santa Fe on February 28 and reached Fort Union in early March to join those men who had arrived earlier. By the time he reached Fort Union, Simpson had already lost eight enlisted men through desertion. Several disappeared shortly after signing up with him in Taos and never even arrived in Santa Fe to be mustered-in. Private Pedro Archuleta, however, was mustered in in Santa Fe on November 23, 1863, a week after his enlistment in Taos and he received a $25 bounty. Apparently it took only a little more than a month's service to convince Archuleta that he was not cut out for military life. On December 21 he deserted from Fort Union and seemed to disappear from sight. For almost 2 years he

evaded discovery but on September 4, 1865, the long arm of military law finally caught up with him at Golondrinas, New Mexico. Archuleta was returned to Fort Union and jailed. He was court-martialed and ordered confined "at Hard labor in charge of the Guard for two years wearing a twenty-four pound ball attached to his left leg by a chain three feet long and to forfeit all pay now due and to become due him, except just dues of the Sutler and Laundress: and at the expiration of his term of confinement to have his head shaved; and to be drummed out of the service." The punishment, however, appears not to have been meted out, for Archuleta's individual records show he was discharged several months later, on November 27, by reason of General Order 50, Department of Missouri in St. Louis, but gave no clue as to the type of discharge.

In January, 1864, three more men who had enlisted in Taos and had been sent to Fort Union to await arrival of the company also deserted. One, Private Juan Domingo Martin, who had been born in Valencia just south of Albuquerque, left after serving a little less than 2 months. Amazingly enough, he decided a month later, on February 29, to join Company K of the New Mexico volunteers which was also stationed at Fort Union. He was successful with his deception for 2 months but was finally discovered and returned to Company I on May 1, shortly before the company was to leave for duty in Arizona.

February saw desertions of two more members of Company I from Fort Union. One of the men was later apprehended, returned to duty, and served with the company until it was disbanded in 1866, at which time he was transferred to the Battalion of New Mexico Volunteers for further duty.

These eight desertions all took place before the company was officially enrolled and were probably due, in great part, to confusion on the part of the enlistees. All official orders

45

and documents were executed in a language they didn't know, the traditions and regulations of the military establishment were totally foreign to their cultural background, and conditions were in a state of flux with the concurrent recruiting and organization of a number of companies to make up the regiment. The next few months would bring the loss of eight more men by desertion but after that, as the men became integrated into a working unit and after the company left northern New Mexico, the desertions stopped.

Within 2 weeks of his arrival at Fort Union with his company, Captain Simpson was sent back to Taos to procure a supply of flour and meat to help feed the infantry volunteers stationed at the fort. The rations were to be paid for by company commanders from savings they had on hand from their respective companies.[7] This trip back to his home territory for foodstuffs prevented Simpson from attending a court-martial at Fort Sumner on March 21 where he was apparently expected to serve on the board.[8] The influx of the many newly organized volunteer companies raised the troop strength at Fort Union to 578 men in March, 1864, and evidently additional supplies were needed, hence Simpson's trip to Taos.[9]

April 11 was, for some reason, a day when wanderlust hit three privates of Company I. One of the men was apprehended 5 months later, long after Company I was on duty in Arizona. He was put into confinement at Fort Union for 4½ months and then transferred to Company G of the volunteers. The last desertion from Company I while it was stationed at Fort Union took place on April 24, after the company had received its orders dispatching them to Arizona. Apparently Private Jose Mestes of Taos decided he didn't want to leave New Mexico and he slipped away from Fort Union.

After approximately only 6 weeks of training at Fort Union, Company I received orders on April 18, along with Company A of the same regiment, to prepare to go on active field duty as part of the Apache Expedition in Arizona.[10] General James H. Carleton, commander of the Department of New Mexico, had decided, in April, to use the two New Mexico companies as part of a force he was organizing against the Apache Indians of southern Arizona. Carleton was taking this action in response to a number of complaints he had received in letters from Governor Goodwin of Arizona and from Lieutenant Colonel Nelson H. Davis, assistant inspector general of the U.S. Army, who had written from Fort Whipple, Arizona. Carleton stated that a private letter, written to him on April 4 by Govenor Goodwin "shews [sic] that there is an immediate and pressing necessity for a military force to go to that country to punish the Indians who are not only numerous but very hostile."[11]

Carleton was aware, however, that not all citizens of the Arizona Territory would approve of his plans for military intervention against the Indians so, to forestall the criticism he felt would come, he wrote to the Army's Adjutant General in Washington citing his plans and reasons for organizing the expedition against the Apaches. Stating that the war against the Navajos was near a final ending, and he hoped to be as fortunate with his campaign against the Apaches, Carleton speculated that perhaps "the great drain upon the treasury which has been kept up by these Indian wars, will forever cease."[12]

Carleton's strategy was to set up a force of 500 infantry and cavalrymen at a post to be constructed on the Gila River in southeastern Arizona, about half way between the present-day towns of Globe and Safford. Carleton ordered that the post be named Fort Goodwin in honor of the Arizona governor and said that the troops were to be sent out to march against the Indians "in every direction to points where the enemy may be found."[13] Simultaneous with this operation, which was to be under the command of Colonel Edwin A. Rigg of the First Infantry, California Volunteers, he planned that other detachments of soldiers would be sent northward from Tucson, southward to the Chiricahua Mountains from Fort Bowie, and southeasterly from Fort Whipple. At the same time, he planned that troops from a number of posts and forts in northwestern and southwestern New Mexico would move against the Apaches in their territory so the combined effect would be the simultaneous harrassment of all the southern Apaches of the various tribes, the Chiricahua, the Gila, the Mogollon, and the Mimbres.

To supplement this campaign, which Carleton hoped would throw the Apaches into a state of panic and confusion, and leave them nowhere to run, Carleton requested that the governor of Arizona send parties of miners out at the same time and he made arrangements to use four parties of 50 men each, made up of Pima and Maricopa Indians, hereditary enemies of the Apaches, which he supplied with arms and ammunition.

In addition, to forestall an escape route into Mexico for the Indians, Carleton informed the governors of the Mexican states of Chihuahua and Sonora of his proposed movements and requested that they put a few hundred of their militia in the field against "this common enemy" and granted them authority to "come over the line into our territory in pursuit of Apaches, when, where and as far as they please."[14]

Carleton was planning what he called "a general war" against the Apaches, saying, "an earnest effort must be made not only to punish them for their continued murders, accompanied as many of those murders have been by burnings at the stake, and by tortures of the most atrocious character:—but either by their removal to a Reservation or by the utter extermination of their men, to ensure a lasting peace, and a security of life to all those who go to that country to search for the precious metals."[15]

The main force for this Apache Expedition against the Indians was to be made up of seven companies of the California Volunteers and Company I of the New Mexico Volunteers. Company A, which left Fort Union with Company I and traveled down the Rio Grande to Las Cruces, and then westward to Arizona with it, was to be used to garrison Fort Bowie. Of the two New Mexico companies chosen for duty in Arizona, Company I was surely far less trained in military procedures and methods than its sister company A which had been at Fort Union, operating as an integrated unit three months longer than I, having arrived there in early December, 1863.[16]

During the last half of April and the first week of May, 1864, after receiving his orders, Captain Simpson began to requisition clothing, camp, and garrison equipment his company would be allowed in accordance with requirements of the Department of New Mexico (see list of equipment requisitioned, page 30, Addendum to Company A) as the men prepared to leave Fort Union along with Company A and march to Las Cruces, the southernmost major settlement on the Rio Grande in New Mexico.

During the first week of May, as Company I prepared for transfer to Arizona, several changes took place in personnel. On May 2, Private Manuel Urban, whose age was listed as 34, but whose hair was described as "grizzly," was transferred to Company K of the volunteers. Urban, apparently not happy with his new company was to desert 3 months later. On May 7, the day Company I was to depart from Fort Union, Private Jose Manuel Aragon wrote a letter requesting that he be transferred from Company C of the volunteers, which was also stationed at Fort Union at the time, into Company I. He stated the reason for his request was that his father and brother were both serving in

47

Company I and he wished to go with them. His request was honored but a check of the personnel listings of Company I brings up several interesting points, including a graphic example of the extremely poor record keeping in regard to the Spanish names. Jose's name is listed as Manuel Arajon on the company roster while his younger brother Jesus' name is spelled Arragon and the third man, and only other one in the company with the same surname, is listed as Pedro Antonio Aragon. Other documents show that Jose's name actually was Aragon and if his request was valid, the third man must be his father. However, Pedro's age is listed as 36, while the two sons are 22 and 24. The most probable explanation of this discrepancy is that the father, who was the last of the three to enlist, had lied about his age, an apparently not uncommon practice of older men who desired to join the volunteers.

When Company I left Fort Union, Private Mileton Ocania remained behind, too ill to travel. Less than a month later, on June 3, he died at the age of 21 from tuberculosis.

On May 7, 1864, the two New Mexico Volunteer companies began their long trek to Las Cruces, 643.6 kilometers (400 miles) away. Las Cruces was headquarters for the Apache Expedition and the "staging area" for movement of troops and supplies to Arizona.

The day after the company set out, Captain Simpson received shocking news. Two of the enlisted men he had singled out to promote to corporal, men he had expected to depend upon, deserted at Las Vegas, New Mexico, the first major town the company approached on its march southward. Peter Frank, a 30-year-old native of Baden, Germany, and Corporal Juan de los Reyes Gonzales, 28, of Taos, both had enlisted in December and had been promoted together on March 1. Records show no further mention of the two men but Frank would surely have been an easy physical specimen to spot among the Mexican population

with his 175 centimeter (5-foot, 10-inch) height, his auburn hair, and blue eyes.

Although Simpson must have been shaken by these desertions, he was still to suffer several more losses. On May 11 one private disappeared when the company was in the area of the Pecos River on their way south and 15 days later, near the village of Luis Lopez on the Rio Grande just south of Socorro, another private who decided he didn't want to fight Apaches left the company.

When the two companies left Fort Union and marched southwest toward Albuquerque as a battalion, Captain Nicolas Quintana of Company A was in command by virtue of his date of rank. However, he soon detoured to Santa Fe to handle some business, leaving Captain Simpson in charge for the march to Tijeras Canyon near Albuquerque, and from there southward along the Rio Grande. Simpson, therefore, was in command at the time when two prisoners tried to escape near Belen and were shot. (For details of the incident see page 5, Company A.)

The long march toward Las Cruces caused Company I to lose another of its men, this time not to desertion but to disability. Second Lieutenant Edward E. Ayer had apparently made a mistake when he transferred from the cavalry to the infantry, even though it had meant a promotion. A deformity of his left foot, which had caused him no trouble as a horse soldier, prevented him from marching long distances. By the time the company had marched the approximately 530 kilometers (330 miles) to Fort Craig, Ayer, and Simpson as well, were aware that Lieutenant Ayer would not be able to carry out his duties. On May 27, in a sworn statement, Captain Simpson stated that "he (Ayer) has been unable, every time he has attempted to walk more than a mile or two at a time, with left foot, and that I have examined it and found it deformed and that to such an extent that it unfits him for duties of an

Infantry officer."[17] The following day the Fort Craig surgeon examined Ayer and concurred that the foot deformity prevented his marching and recommended a disability pension. Three days later Ayer resigned and the company continued southward with only two officers.

On June 6, in Santa Fe, a replacement for Ayer was commissioned. He was Joseph Felmer, a 31-year-old sergeant of the First California Cavalry who was discharged in order to enable him to accept the commission as second lieutenant in the New Mexico volunteers. On June 9, Felmer was ordered to leave Santa Fe and to "proceed with all practicable dispatch to join his Company."[18] Before Felmer could leave General Carleton received word that an officer and several members of a military party escorting 750 captured Navajos to the Bosque Redondo reservation from Arizona had left the Navajos alone in Tijeras Canyon east of Albuquerque while they went into town to enjoy its pleasures. Although none of the Indians escaped, Carleton was furious and relieved the officer of his command and immediately dispatched Felmer to replace him. Felmer successfully escorted the Navajo prisoners to Fort Sumner on July 2, 1864. Proceeding to Arizona, he eventually arrived at Fort Goodwin on August 25, after being held for some time on detached duty at Fort Bowie.[19]

While the two New Mexico companies were marching downriver enroute to Las Cruces, the main force of the Apache Expedition was already moving out, in several groups, on the way to Arizona. Five companies of California volunteer infantrymen, one company of California volunteer cavalrymen, the beef cattle to provision the expedition, and Colonel Rigg, expedition commander, all left Las Cruces in late May. The bulk of the stores to provision the company still remained at Las Cruces, due to lack of transportation, although one train of supplies was dispatched westward under contract to a well-known civilian merchant, Estevan Ochoa.[20] The several groups of men and supplies took different routes through southeastern Arizona but finally all rendezvoused at a spot on the Gila River where they set up a temporary camp and supply depot which they called Camp Goodwin. Within a few days after his arrival there, Colonel Rigg received orders detailing the exact location where he was to set up the permanent fort in an area approximately 53 kilometers (33 miles) to the northwest in the valley of the Tularosa. While the bulk of the men remained at the temporary camp, Colonel Rigg and several companies of men began laying out the site of the permanent fort.

Company I and Company A, weary after the long march from Fort Union, must have been disconcerted to learn, on their arrival at Las Cruces on June 4, that they were ordered to leave for Arizona at noon on June 6. This tight schedule left insufficient time for all preparations to be made so another order was issued, delaying departure of the battalion until 4 o'clock in the morning of June 8.[21] During the brief layover the men were rationed and issued 100 rounds of ammunition each. Major Thomas Blakeney, of the First California Cavalry, who was to command the battalion on its march to Arizona, issued an order which said the laundresses, who usually traveled with the companies, could not accompany the command. He directed that company commanding officers issue the women papers with which they could draw rations at Las Cruces while the unit was away.[22] Four California volunteers who were prisoners in confinement at the Las Cruces headquarters, were put under the command of Captain Simpson on June 7.[23] They were to accompany Company I to Arizona where Simpson was to deliver them to their proper company commanders.

In the early morning darkness, probably grumbling and stumbling, the men of Company I left Las Cruces and marched westward into Arizona. Their route took them through rough terrain that often provided little forage for the supply-wagon animals and little good water. On June 16, after camping at a watering hole, probably in southeastern Arizona, the two companies split up. Company A proceeded to Fort Bowie accompanied by 11 men from Company I who, under the command of a California infantry volunteer sergeant, escorted them to their destination. Once Company A's supplies had been unloaded at Fort Bowie, the detachment of Company I men would bring the emptied wagons on to Camp Goodwin.[24]

Four days later, on June 20, 1864, Lieutenant Mann, Sergeant Charles Hynes, Corporals Victor Medina and Antonio Ma Romero, along with 12 privates of Company I were ordered to retrace their steps and march back to the Rio Mimbres in New Mexico, west of Fort Cummings.[25] The weary men were assigned to escort a supply train to safeguard it from possible Indian attack. After they left, remnants of the decimated company proceeded on to Camp Goodwin, arriving on June 23, the day that Colonel Rigg had sent some trains and the ambulance to Camp Goodwin to begin transferring the troops to the permanent fort.[26]

While the transfer of men and equipment was taking place, and while brush huts were being constructed at Fort Goodwin, Company I remained at the temporary camp on the banks of the Gila, still under command of Major Blakeney, who was in charge of Camp Goodwin.

On July 2, Colonel Rigg notified Major Blakeney that transportation had been sent to the camp to move all remaining stores there.[27] Rigg ordered that Blakeney break camp but told him to place a party in ambush around the site so that if Indians came in to scavenge after his command had left, they could be surprised and killed.

Company I assisted with the last of the loading and left Camp Goodwin on July 4. While they were working to break camp, men at the permanent camp were celebrating Independence Day. All labor was suspended for the holiday, the troops paraded, a volley of muskets was fired, the American flag was elevated on a temporary flag-staff, and a Fourth of July address was given.[28] Company I arrived at Fort Goodwin on July 6 and this last short march to their destination must have seemed easy after the 1126 kilometers (700-mile) trek from Fort Union to the Gila River.

Post returns list Fort Goodwin as being officially established on June 21, 1864. It was situated about 4 kilometers (2.5 miles) from the Gila River about 193 kilometers (120 miles) from Fort Bowie and 120 miles from Tucson. The only means of communication available with the rest of the world was by military express riders. The valley of the Tularosa, where Fort Goodwin was built, was described by Colonel Rigg as "the most beautiful one I have seen in Arizona."[29] He stated that a spring which "heads far up and furnishes water sufficient to irrigate all the lands fit to be cultivated" was found up toward the mountains. At the lower end of the valley he discovered, on the west side of the stream, "fine shade made by large mesquite trees...the largest of the species I have ever seen. Some of them are as large and wide-spreading as the oak."[30] He ordered a survey done to define the boundaries and limits of Fort Goodwin to be 15 square kilometers (6 miles square) in area with the site of the fort as the center. Corrals were built to contain the beef cattle, tents were pitched and store rooms built to house supplies. Rigg ordered, however, that none of the ash or walnut trees in the valley should be cut, showing an apparent appreciation for the slower-growing hardwoods.

Even before Company I arrived at Fort Goodwin, Rigg had already ordered three separate commands of men out on Indian scouts in the surrounding area. Ten days after their arrival at the fort, it was Company I's turn to receive orders, on July 16, to take to the field. Several days earlier Lieutenant Colonel King Woolsey of the Arizona Volunteers, commanding a troop of 76 Arizona miners who had been out scouting for Indians, reported to Colonel Rigg that he had discovered 12 hectares (30 acres) of wheat and about 16 hectares (40 acres) of corn on Pinal Creek which had been cultivated by the Apaches. Rigg decided to send a force to the area to destroy the crops since the wheat was ripe and he desired to prevent the Indians from harvesting and caching it in the mountains for winter use.

Rigg ordered Company I, along with Company E, Fifth Infantry California Volunteers, and a detachment of Company E, First Cavalry California Volunteers to proceed down the Gila River to where the San Carlos empties into it.[31] There, the detachment, under the command of Major Blakeney, was to proceed about 19 kilometers (12 miles) up the San Carlos to the point where some corn fields would be found. They were also ordered to establish a depot there from which the soldiers could carry out short expeditions, of 8 days or less, into the surrounding countryside against the Indians. In this way the men could carry all the rations they needed in their haversacks, travel lightly, and thus fulfill General Carleton's plan which he had expressed when he wrote:

> We *must* trust to the gallantry of small parties against any numbers. Large parties move snail-like; are seen at once and are avoided—generally are laughed at by these Apaches. Small parties move secretly; cover more ground; move with celerity; emulate to do better than all others; and in the end either destroy, or worry the Indians into submission.[32] *Every party, in energy, perseverance, resolution, and self-denial, must strive to outdo all other parties.*[33]

The soldiers left Fort Goodwin on July 18 at 5 o'clock in the afternoon, with their musket barrels blackened as ordered by Colonel Rigg.[34] They marched northwest until they reached the Gila River. The command continued in a northwesterly direction, camping during the day, breaking camp at sunset, and traveling during the nighttime hours in an attempt to avoid discovery. By 2 o'clock on the morning of July 23, they had reached their destination on the San Carlos. They made a camp which they named Camp Rigg in honor of the commanding officer of Fort Goodwin and sent out scouts to ascertain whether or not Indians were in the area. Some corn fields found in the vicinity were destroyed and during the next few days, while awaiting arrival of their slower-moving supply train, several more Indian scouts were made, each time with the men supplied with cooked rations in their haversacks. However, no Indians were found.[35]

On July 25, Major Blakeney sent some troops to gather and bundle up corn fodder from the destroyed fields to be hauled into camp for the expedition's animals to eat when they were corraled at night. The same day the supply train arrived and Blakeney prepared to mount a scout against Apaches at a rancheria on Pinal Creek. Detachments from each of the companies were ordered to stay behind at the base camp, under the command of one of the California captains who was sick. The rest of the men were rationed for 16 days, with the first 3 day's rations cooked and carried in their packs.[36]

Apparently Captain Simpson was originally expected to remain behind while his men, under Lieutenant Mann, would go on the scout. However, he applied for permission to accompany the scout and was allowed to do so.[37]

The troops left camp at four the next afternoon and marched to Jaycox's Spring, 12 kilometers (eight miles) west of Camp Rigg. There they stopped and made camp but were not allowed to light fires. They remained at Jaycox's Spring until 5 p.m. the next evening

51

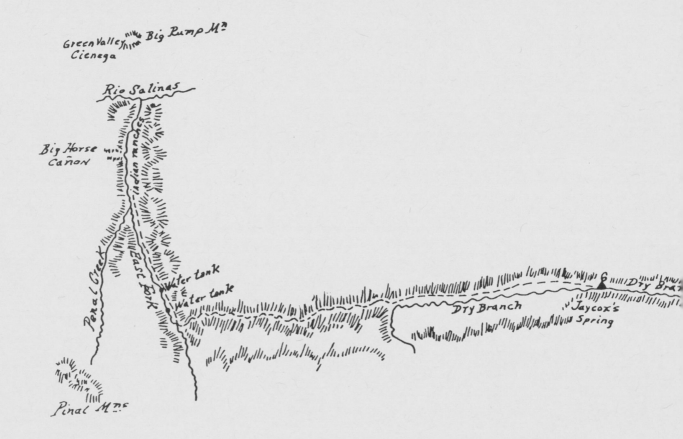

Expedition to the Pinal Mountains, Ariz. Territory
July 18 — August 7, 1864

NOTE: This map was submitted, as part of his official report, by Major Thomas J. Blakeney,
First California Cavalry, on August 8, 1864.
The report can be found in War of the Rebellion, *Series 1, Vol. 41, Book 1, pp. 81–86.*
The map, of course, was missing.

Courtesy National Archives, Wash., D.C.

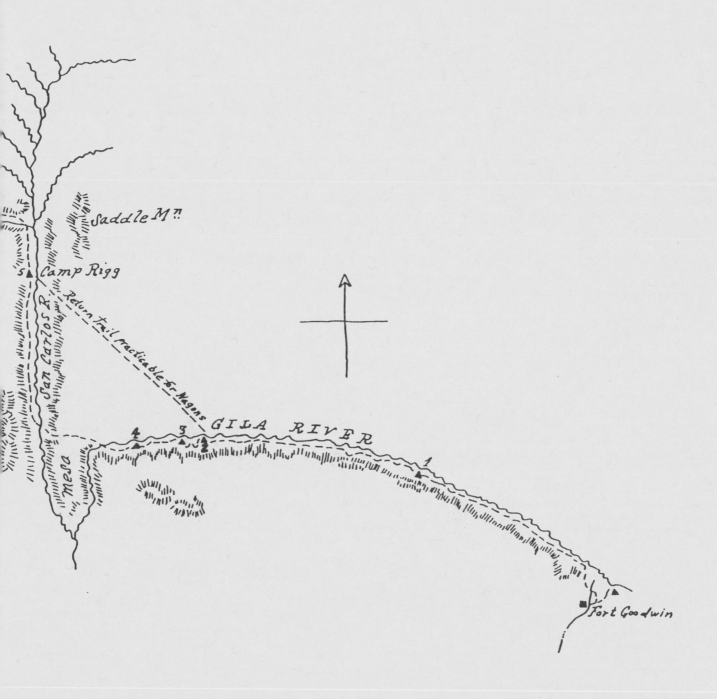

when they took up the line of march for Pinal Creek, expecting to reach it in 8 hour's march so they would be in position to employ a surprise attack on the Apache rancheria at daybreak. Before leaving the spring, Major Blakeney ordered Company I's Lieutenant Mann to take a detachment of men, and the pack train loaded with supplies for the command, and set off on a less direct trail for Pinal Creek. This way the foot soldiers could travel quickly and more quietly, directly toward their objective, with less chance of discovery and yet be assured that the supplies would arrive the next day.

Henry H. Jaycox, a 28-year-old miner, after whom the spring was named, was the guide for the troops but the night was very dark and the trail difficult to follow. Several times the expedition lost the trail and finally Jaycox decided to merely lead them in the right direction without concern for whether or not

54

they remained on the trail. In the blackness the men could scarcely see one another and at about midnight they unfortunately stumbled across a temporary camp of Apaches which was situated in a deep ravine. The startled Indians scattered and quickly sent off several messengers to warn their people at the rancheria. Fearful that the main body of Indians would be forewarned of their coming, Major Blakeney pushed his men forward in a heavy march over the rough and rocky country through the darkness, not allowing them to stop until sunrise when they found some water tanks at which they could refresh themselves and their animals. At this point fresh tracks of two Apaches, less than 30 minutes old, were found, confirming Blakeney's suspicion that the Indians had indeed sent some runners to alert the Apache camp. Blakeney urged the men on but by 8:30 a.m. they were so worn out with fatigue he was forced to halt for 2 hours to allow them

Apache Rancherea
Author's Collection

to rest. It was not until noon that the troops finally arrived at the spring and Indian rancheria which had been their destination.

The march had taken considerably longer than Blakeney had originally anticipated and the bad luck of encountering the Indian party during the night had eliminated any chance of taking the Apaches unaware. When the men of Company I, and their comrades, arrived at the upper spring they endured the embarrassment of being shouted at and taunted by the Indians who were safely ensconced, out of reach, on the very tops of the high, rocky ridges bordering the creek.

Aware that it was useless to try to reach the Indians, Major Blakeney ordered the cavalrymen to charge a little group of wicki-ups near the spring, but the Indians had thoroughly evacuated the shanties, and removed all their belongings. Blakeney had no choice but to continue the march past the jeering Indians, maintaining some semblance of dignity by having the troops appear to ignore them. They halted at the old camping ground nearby which had been used by Colonel Woolsey's party of miners some time earlier. Then Blakeney sent some infantrymen to the Indian village to search it and take possession of any property they might find there. At this point the Indians, on the rocky cliffs overhanging the valley, hoisted a white truce flag. When the infantry officer responded in kind, three Indians, including a squaw, came down and expressed a desire to talk. The squaw told Major Blakeney the Indians were aware that campaigns were being made against the Apaches from all sides and that her people had no desire to fight. Blakeney told her that he wanted to talk to the whole band together with their chief, not just individual Indians. She went away with a promise that she would bring the chief and the band in and that they would surrender.

Her promise was not carried out. The next day a total of only nine Indians appeared in camp, wandering in at various times, so that there were never more than two or three in camp at a time. The Apaches were probably only satisfying their curiosity about the soldiers under the safety of the truce.

That day, July 29, Company I's Lieutenant Mann arrived with the pack train of supplies. Apparently the strain and responsibility of bringing the pack train through the rugged, Indian-infested country for 2 days and nights, possibly combined with residual fatigue caused by his long march back to the Rio Mimbres and then on to Fort Goodwin earlier in the month, affected Mann, causing a sort of "combat fatigue." Whatever the cause, it was reported to Major Blakeney that Mann was showing signs of insanity after his arrival; that he was imagining he was being followed through camp by an Indian and that Mr. Parker, the other guide with the expedition, was trying to kill him.[38] Blakeney wrote in his report that night, "Tonight Lieutenant Mann was wandering through camp perfectly wild, and I was compelled to put him under guard for fear he might do some injury either to himself or someone else."[39] No further mention of Mann's condition is contained in the reports and he apparently recovered, for he continued on duty with his company without further incident.

Another event occurred the same day which was to have more serious repercussions. That afternoon a young Indian boy came into camp and stated that he desired to remain there and live with the soldiers. He said that he was an orphan and wanted to become a white man "to have a hat, and boots, and clothes."[40] Blakeney seems to have been quite taken by the boy who he described as about 14 years old and with "a smart, intelligent look for an Indian."[41] Blakeney allowed the boy to remain in camp, saw that he was given all the food he could eat,

55

promised that he could stay in camp, and told the youth he would be taken away with the troops when they left.

For several more days the Indians continued to come into camp in small groups and then return to the tribe. One group of six was led by Chief Crooked Foot. Although he, and others, talked of an awareness that Apaches were being hunted all over the area simultaneously, and spoke of being compelled to submit sooner or later, the Apaches still held back and did not commit themselves to a mass surrender.

On July 31, the 14th day the scouting party had been in the field, an old squaw came into the camp and demanded the young Indian boy who had remained there, saying he was hers. Blakeney asked the boy if he wanted to leave but the boy said no. The squaw then asked for a "present" in exchange for the youth but when Blakeney questioned the boy he said that she had no claim on him and that no gift should be made to her on his account. After assuring the squaw that the boy was not a captive, but free to leave any time, Blakeney sent the old woman away, disgruntled. About noonday the boy went down to the cornfield to pick some corn and was seized there by some of the Apaches who kidnapped him and carried him off. On learning of the incident, Blakeney seized, as hostages, six of the Indians who were in camp at the moment and sent another Indian out to demand the return of the boy. The Indian returned some time later with a blanket but without the boy. Blakeney refused the blanket and sent the Indian back. At sundown, when no further word had come from the Apaches, Blakeney ordered the six captives, two bucks, two boys, and two squaws, tied for the night. While the soldiers were in the process of carrying out his orders, one of the Indian women attempted to escape and was shot and killed by the guard. In the excitement, one of the boy hostages, about 15 years of age, also started to run. As he ran into the extremely heavy brush

surrounding the camp, about 20 shots were fired at him. It was assumed that he was also killed since the Indians were heard, for the next several nights, searching the brush for his body.

The incident apparently changed Blakeney's attitude and he no longer tried to parley with the Indians. The next day he sent Captain Simpson and Company I to scout over the mountains to the south of the canyon, looking for Indians. Other units were sent in all directions with orders to kill all buck Indians big enough to bear arms and to capture all squaws and children, while also searching for caches of wheat. Blakeney, himself, went with a company of California infantry volunteers to scour the area. His men killed one Apache, which they later discovered to be a squaw, and captured another woman. The other troops found no Indians although several caches of food were discovered.

That day Lt. Colonel Woolsey and his miners arrived at the camp and, that night, at Woolsey's suggestion, Major Blakeney freed the remaining squaw he had been holding as hostage. Blakeney told her he wanted her to bring the Apache chief into camp and gave her instructions to inform the tribe that unless the kidnapped boy was returned to him he would kill the remaining hostages he held. The squaw left, promising to return within 2 days with the chief.

While Blakeney and his troops were having their problems with the Pinal Creek Indians, other events were taking place back at Fort Goodwin of which they were unaware. Colonel Rigg had made plans to send two more infantry companies and the balance of the California cavalry company up to their area to increase the troop strength.[42] These additional troops were to set up a depot on the San Carlos, have Blakeney's command join them there, and outfit a large expedition against Indians in the vicinity. Major Joseph Smith of the Fifth

Infantry California Volunteers, who would lead these supplemental troops to the San Carlos, was to take over command of the whole expedition and replace Major Blakeney as leader. It was ordered that some of the men would be left behind at the supply depot on the San Carlos when the expedition took to the field and that these men would collect all the Indian grain they could find in the area, store it in wagons, and send it back to Fort Goodwin where it was needed. Smith, and the additional troops, left Fort Goodwin and began the march to the San Carlos on July 28, the day Blakeney's command first entered the Indian village on Pinal Creek.

Blakeney, however, was not yet aware of this impending change. By August 2 he had ordered all his troops at Pinal Creek on half rations in order to conserve food so that he could outfit a scouting expedition to Big Rump Valley, 32 kilometers (20 miles) away, where he believed a large number of Apaches were concentrated to resist the soldiers.[43] Blakeney expected a big fight there. As part of his preparations, he ordered details out to cut the Indian corn and dry it to supplement the men's meagre rations.

The following day, Blakeney waited all day for the Apaches to return the kidnapped boy to his camp as a result of his ultimatum. At sundown, when it became obvious they were not going to comply, he ordered the two Indian men hostages hung. During that same day Blakeney apparently received the Special Orders telling him of the impending arrival of Major Smith's troops and the change in command.

Blakeney, however, decided to go ahead with the Indian scouts he had been preparing for the previous several days. The next morning, August 4, he ordered a California infantry company to march up Pinal Creek to the Pinal Mountains and ordered Captain Simpson and 40 men of Company I to the same destination by way of Big Horse Canyon. He also prepared to lead a small detachment himself by another route.

A short time after the California infantrymen had set out from the camp, and just as Company I was preparing to leave, an express rider arrived with a dispatch from Fort Goodwin which ordered all troops to come in from the field and return to the fort. When Blakeney received this news he immediately sent a dispatch to the company which had just left for the Pinal Mountains, ordering them to return to camp.

The sudden change in plans had come about when Colonel Rigg, at Fort Goodwin, had received orders by special express instructing him to send a number of California troops, including much of his staff, into Las Cruces by August 31 to be mustered out of the service.[44] He had dispatched Smith's troops from the fort just 6 days earlier but now all plans for the big expedition had to be abandoned and all the troops, not just the affected California volunteers, had to be recalled from the field.

The following day, on August 5, Blakeney ordered the troops to destroy all the corn and other crops remaining in the area. After this was done he broke camp at 2 p.m. and started his march back to Camp Rigg on the San Carlos.[45] He left behind 12 men of Company I, along with 12 men of Company E, Fifth Infantry California Volunteers, and three volunteers from Woolsey's miners, under command of a sergeant. These men were ordered to hide about the camp to ambush and kill any Indians who might come into the camp site to search for anything left behind after departure of the command.

Approximately 3 hours after the troops had left, about 15 Apaches approached the camp. When they were within 27 meters (30 yards) of the hidden soldiers, the men fired upon them. The Indians were thrown into confusion and fled in every direction, dropping

57

their weapons. The soldiers started in pursuit but the Indians disappeared into the thick brush surrounding the camp. The men found one dead Indian and trailed four others into the brush by following blood stains, but were unable to locate them. The sergeant in charge of the party reported his certainty that five Indians were either killed or mortally wounded and reported recovering two blankets, one lance, one bow, several arrows, and two pairs of moccasins which the Apaches had dropped in their hasty retreat. The detachment then left the area, rejoined their command at daybreak the next day and made their way back to Camp Rigg with the rest of the unit.

The net result of the whole Pinal Creek expedition was summed up by Major Blakeney as follows: Indians killed—10; Indians captured—2; amount of corn destroyed—20 acres plus a considerable amount of beans, pumpkins, etc.[46] The results, when considered against the expense in money and hardship, of putting so many men in the field for a long period of time, could hardly have been what General Carleton had hoped for when making his grandiose plans for defeat of the Apaches. Even Colonel Woolsey's miners, who were in the field against the Indians for 87 days, failed to kill a single Apache on their expedition but did lose one of their men who left camp by himself, "was waylaid by six Indians, shot through the chest with a rifle, lanced, stripped and left for dead."[47]

Colonel Rigg was also displeased with the results of the expedition. He wrote, in his report to Carleton's headquarters in Santa Fe, that he had heard that Major Blakeney "was not successful in accomplishing what he was sent to do" and went on to say, "I cannot help but state that he at least exercised bad judgement....His zeal for an Indian boy resulted in stampeding the whole rancheria."[48] Rigg was referring to the fact that once the Indian boy had been kidnapped and Blakeney had taken

hostages, the Indians discontinued their visits to the camp and all discussions of possible surrender to the troops. Rigg also wrote, "This is my opinion, that if Major Smith or Colonel Woolsey had arrived in time, from 200 to 500 Apaches would have come in." While this is pure speculation on the part of Colonel Rigg, it is true that King Woolsey had promised that he would join Major Blakeney at Pinal Creek on the 30th of July and had not done so until August 1, 1864, after the boy had been kidnapped and the hostages shot while trying to escape.[49]

As a final note to the whole incident, when Colonel Rigg left Fort Goodwin on August 11, on his way to Las Cruces to be mustered out as ordered, the one remaining hostage of the Pinal Creek incident, a young Apache boy, was put in his charge. Apparently the boy was to be transported to Las Cruces. The captured boy appeared, in Rigg's words, "well contented, and showed no disposition to get away, and was apparently much attached to my servant."[50] However, on the fourth or fifth night of Rigg's trip eastward, the boy escaped and Rigg conjectured that the youth had recognized the locality and that perhaps some of his people were in the vicinity.

The men from Company I, along with the rest of the expedition, arrived back at Fort Goodwin on August 7 at 11:30 p.m. They had been gone a month on their scout to the Pinal Creek and had traveled 402 kilometers (250 miles).[51]

One interesting question is raised by the investigation of the records pertaining to the Pinal Creek expedition. In his declaration for an invalid pension, made in 1892, Captain Simpson claimed that he had suffered a gunshot wound to the left leg while traveling from the San Carlos River to Pinal Creek, Arizona Territory, on or about July 24, 1865. The pension claim stated that he had been ambushed on the road while in command of his troops and that the ball had splintered and four fragments had entered his leg near the ankle caus- ing injury to the Achilles' tendon. Simpson claimed he had been treated by the surgeon at Fort Goodwin, Doctor J. D. Cox, and investiga- tion shows that a physician by that name was indeed stationed at the fort. Simpson claimed that as a result of the wound he had suffered partial paralysis and loss of sensation in his left leg and foot.

On preliminary investigation, the claim might appear spurious. The year is obviously wrong; Simpson was in the described area in July, 1864, but not in 1865. The official report of the expedition, written by Major Blakeney, makes no mention of any ambush or of any injury to Captain Simpson. In all the reports of the Apache Expedition made by Colonel Rigg and also in Blakeney's report of the Pinal Creek scout, no mention is made of the Indians hav- ing any firearms, only bows and arrows and lances. And War Department records on Simpson have no entry which show either the company or Simpson being in action on July 24, 1865, nor any mention of Simpson's wound or treatment.

However, further investigation of the mat- ter opens up the possibility that Simpson's claim may well have been true. First of all, Simpson had apparently already been wounded by a gunshot in the right leg in 1855 in an Indian fight against the Utes while serv- ing as a sergeant in a New Mexico Mounted Volunteer company.[52] An old friend and neighbor of Simpson's, Aloys Schewrich, swore in an affidavit that in 1855 he saw him at the hospital at Fort Massachusetts where Simpson had a gunshot wound in the right leg dressed. Schewrich said that Simpson had received the wound in an Indian fight at Cerhancha Saguache, a spot 137 kilometers (85 miles) north of Taos, which was then part of New Mexico Territory but which has since become a part of the state of Colorado. War Department records do note that Simpson lost his pistol in a

fight at Cerhancha, apparently at the time he was wounded.[53] This one wound should have been sufficient for his claim and inventing a second injury would have been unnecessary. But Schewrich further swore that when Simpson returned to Taos in 1866, after com- manding Company I in Arizona, he showed him another wound "below the ankle in left leg received in an Indian fight during the late war."[54] Simpson also filled in a Bureau of Pen- sions descriptive form in which he listed iden- tifying marks which included "4 scars on right leg, 3 scars on left leg."[55]

The matter of the wrong year on the pen- sion document appears to be a mere typo- graphical error, a simple slip of memory 28 years later, or a slip of the tongue, for the month and location seem right. While it is true that no mention of injury to Captain Simpson is made in the two official reports submitted by Colonel Rigg and Major Blakeney, by the same token, no accidental injuries or illnesses suf- fered by any of the other men is mentioned either, with the exception of Lieutenant Mann's temporary derangement and the note that a Captain Wellman was left in charge of the sup- ply depot because he was sick. Without a doubt, considering the length of the Pinal Creek Ex- pedition and the conditions under which it was carried out, other men must have suffered serious illnesses and various injuries. Both Rigg and Blakeney were California volunteer offi- cers and investigation of large numbers of re- ports by California officers who had New Mexico volunteers serving under them show that they seldom and almost grudgingly men- tioned activities of the New Mexico troops.

The fact that the War Department records fail to mention Simpson's wounds, either in 1855 or 1864, is not at all unusual. It has been found that a great many veterans' records are extremely deficient in this area. Evidently paperwork was not routinely forwarded on such injuries, particularly when they were not

59

life-threatening. Blakeney's mention that Captain Simpson "applied for permission to accompany the scout" as the troops were preparing to leave Camp Rigg for Pinal Creek also could be interpreted as having a bearing on whether or not Simpson had been wounded.[56] Presumably, under normal conditions, Captain Simpson would have led his own company which was included in the scout. Was he being left behind, with the ill Captain Wellman, because of an injury to his leg?

Failure of official reports to mention the fact that the Indians might have had any guns, and thus been able to shoot Captain Simpson, appears not to be pertinent. The Apaches shot and killed one of Woolsey's men on July 25 in the general area.[57] In a report made by Captain Julius C. Shaw of the First New Mexico Cavalry Volunteers, who headed a scout against the Apaches from Fort Wingate, New Mexico, down to the Gila and all the way to Fort Goodwin, at the very same time the Pinal Creek Expedition was in the field, he mentions Indian firearms. While on the San Carlos River, Captain Shaw met with 76 Apache warriors "about one-half of which were armed with rifles and other fire-arms. The balance carried lances and bows and arrows, and some also carried slungshots [sic]."[58] The Apaches told Shaw that they often bought "corn, powder, lead, blankets, etc." from the pueblo of Zuni and also from Mexican traders. After an attack upon the Indians, Shaw even captured five of their rifles. He estimated that the warriors of the Sierra Blanca and vicinity would number from 350 to 400, about one-half of whom were armed with firearms. Shaw also stated that the Apaches claimed the Zunis had told them, after the Navajos had surrendered, the white men killed all the men and made slaves of the women and children. If this belief was widespread among Apaches of the area, it would explain the hesitation of the Indians to surrender to Major Blakeney at Pinal Creek.

On August 19, Private Felipe Romero of Company I, an 18-year-old, died at Fort Goodwin from an unnamed disease.[59] Romero, who had been a member of Lieutenant Mann's detachment which made the long march westward and was then ordered back to the Rio Mimbres, later traveling west again to Fort Goodwin during June and July, left no belongings except the clothing he was buried in. In a list, which was typical of those for deceased privates of the volunteers, the Army noted that his possessions consisted of one pair of infantry trousers, old and valueless; one forage cap, one flannel shirt, and one pair of drawers. No shoes or boots were listed and it is possible that these items, valuable to an infantryman, were issued to another man while he was hospitalized or perhaps even taken by one of them when his death was imminent.

On August 25, Second Lieutenant Felmer finally joined the company, arriving from Fort Bowie where he had been held on detached service.[60] Company I now finally had its full complement of three officers. On August 28, Lieutenant Mann was ordered to escort a government supply train from Fort Goodwin to the Tucson supply sub-depot.[61] Corporal Antonio Ma Romero and Privates Jose Maria Casados, Encarnacion Gonzales, Loretto Gonzales, Jose Encarnacion Marruha, Gabriel P. Mata, Juan Jose Romero, Jose Salazar, and Nestor Tafoya accompanied him.[62] By September 15, Mann and his men returned to Fort Goodwin from the escort but the lieutenant was apparently ill, for the post returns list him as sick.[63] Three days later Lieutenant Felmer was put in charge of an Indian scout and he and his men were rationed for 10 days. The group returned to Fort Goodwin on September 27, after an apparently uneventful search, for the post returns make no mention of any contact with Indians.[64]

By October, 1864, more California volunteers were approaching the end of their enlistment period and would soon be leaving Arizona. On October 6, General Carleton stated that he planned, in 2 days, to order the Fifth Infantry California Volunteers to march away from Fort Goodwin soon, leaving only one company of California cavalry volunteers and Company I at the post.[65] Because of the severe decrease in manpower, he had, earlier in the summer, ordered that the post at Tucson be closed and the supplies in its depot be transferred to Tubac, Fort Bowie, and Fort Goodwin.[66] In the same letter Carleton noted that along with the influx of these supplies, "the troops at Tubac and Fort Goodwin will necessarily have a great deal of scouting to do and a reasonable amount of express service."

In a letter to John Goodwin, governor of Arizona, written several days later, Carleton described his predicament brought about by the loss of a large number of troops. Knowing the area would be desperately undermanned, he wrote:

> From being obliged to muster out of service the California volunteers, it became necessary to recall from the southern portion of Arizona all the troops, except one company of cavalry at Tubac, one company of infantry at Fort Bowie (Company A of the New Mexico volunteers), and one company of cavalry and one of infantry (Company I) at Fort Goodwin. Until I receive additional troops it will be impossible for me to prosecute active operations against the Apaches of Arizona as vigorously as I wish...[67]

Carleton went on to say that residents of the territory should understand "to what straits I am reduced even to garrison important points and protect our material until other troops come to our help" and he stated that he had applied to the War Department for 2,000 more men.

The men in the field continued to carry out their duties with pragmatic perseverence. On October 16, Second Lieutenant Felmer left Fort Goodwin with Sergeant Eugenio Romero, one other noncommissioned officer, and 13 privates of Company I to escort a government train to Fort Cummings, New Mexico.[68] The train was in charge of Benjamin Orea, a civilian wagonmaster, and the men were rationed for 13 days and were to escort the train back to Fort Goodwin once it had been loaded.

On November 12, the men at Fort Goodwin watched the California troops, which Carleton had referred to earlier, march away from the post, on their way to Las Cruces to be mustered out. They must have felt very vulnerable, for now the garrison was reduced to only two companies. When the 4 months' previous average troop strength had been approximately 336 men, the number of soldiers assigned to the fort now dropped to 157.[69]

During the 4 months since Fort Goodwin had been established, the troops had been involved in building the post. When time would permit, between escort duties, Indian scouts, and other activities, work went forward on building corrals, warehouse structures, planting gardens, and the myriad other jobs necessary to improve the installation. Now cold weather was setting in and on November 28, Lieutenant Mann left Fort Goodwin at 8 a.m. with six privates from Company I to march to the Gila River and cut timber to be used in building quarters to replace the original brush huts.[70] The detachment returned to the fort on December 1. Possibly these quarters were constructed of adobe bricks made by the soldiers, for adobe structures were built between the fort's establishment in 1864 and its abandonment in 1871, as evidenced by rows of mounds containing adobe bricks which can be found at the site even today.[71]

The same day that Mann left on the wood-cutting expedition, Lieutenant Felmer captured and brought into the post two Apache Indians described by Major Gorman as "decrepit and old."[72] In December, one of Felmer's

61

Apache captives, a squaw, was released because she had told Major Gorman, the California cavalry volunteer officer in charge of the post, that she would be able to return to the rest of her band and persuade them to come into camp and surrender within 15 days. Apparently, even though they were not yet aware of it, the military "scorched-earth" policy of crop destruction, carried out by soldiers in the area during the previous summer, had been effective and was causing great hardship for Apaches in that section of Arizona. Approximately 3 weeks after the squaw had left, one of the tribe's sub-chiefs arrived at Fort Goodwin, saying he had been sent by the chiefs of two tribes to solicit peace.[73] Major Gorman told him if the Indians were in earnest they would have to bring in their families and lay down their arms. The Indian ambassador acceded to the demands and left the fort to return to his people.

During December construction continued on the fort. On December 9, a noncommissioned officer from the California cavalry volunteers, along with three privates from his company and five men from Company I, was sent to the river to cut poles for further building.[74] Three days later Lieutenant Mann left to lead an escort party to Fort Cummings, a trip that would keep him away from the fort for the better part of a month.[75] Private Jose Maria Casados, of Company I, was one of the soldiers who accompanied him.

On December 29, 1864, Private Antonio Meistes, a 25-year-old native of Taos, died at Fort Goodwin.[76] His death points up the miserable conditions under which the men at the fort were carrying out their duties. Private Meistes, whose name was consistently misspelled on offical military records and is actually Mestes, died of scurvey. (NOTE: The Spanish names of the New Mexico Volunteers are misspelled on the official records with great frequency, i.e. Taffoya for Tafoya, Lobato for Lovato, Baco for Baca, Felis for Feliz, etc. Since the authors cannot assume to correct these names without absolute proof in each case, they have been listed in the company rosters as they appear on the official records. Anyone desiring to further research any of these individuals in the personal records of individual soldiers in the National Archives should be aware of possible variations in name spellings.) Captain Simpson, in filling out a document to aid Mestes' widow, Isabella, to obtain a pension, stated that Mestes had been a healthy man when he entered the service but that while in Arizona, "his (Simpson's) company was entirely deprived of vegetable diet and scurvy and other kindred diseases was the consequence."[77] In a private letter, printed in the *Santa Fe Weekly Gazette,* 4 months later, the author stated, "This command (Fort Goodwin) is suffering very badly from the scurvy," so apparently the problem was of long duration.[78]

Captain Shaw, in reporting his Indian scout from Fort Wingate the previous summer, stated that he had destroyed at least 160 hectartes (400 acres) of Indian crops including corn, beans, wheat, watermelons, muskmelons, and squashes but that he had abstained from destroying any crops along the Tularosa in the vicinity of Fort Goodwin at the request of Colonel Rigg, who obviously wanted to use the Indian plantings to supplement his men's rations.[79] But apparently, once these freshstuffs were used up, the men at Fort Goodwin were unable to obtain any other vegetables in the shipments of supplies which were made to them.

Conditions apparently were very bad. Records are sketchy but Sergeant Eugenio Romero's pension records show that he contracted scurvy in 1865 and became very ill, bleeding at the mouth and vomiting, and that by 1866 the condition had caused him to lose all his teeth.[80] Corporal Reyes Duran's pension records show that he suffered from recurrent bouts of diarrhea during 1865 and 1866.[81] Even the animals were suffering from shortages of foodstuffs. In early April, 1865, Major Gorman stated that there had been no grain at the post in over 5 months and that many of the animals had died.[82] He reported the balance of the horses and mules in such poor condition that "they are unfit for active service in the mountains."[83]

It seems incongruous that soldiers were suffering from scurvey in a valley which Colonel Rigg glowingly described as a beautiful one with an additional 240 hectares (600 acres) north of the spring over to the Gila River which could, with care, be made to produce crops—in addition to the lands nearby which he stated were already fit for growing crops and for gardens. Rigg had also stated that water was abundant and pure and that a fine deposit of salt had been found near the post. During the summer of 1864 the troops had apparently been too busy, both with being away on prolonged Indian scouts and with building the fort, to prepare the ground and do any extensive crop planting. Then, as the growing season passed, the military failed to supply them with grain and vegetables. Groups of Pinal and Coyotero Indians had practically cut off the delivery of supplies to Fort Goodwin.[84] It would not be until October, 1865, that the military would move five companies of men to Fort Grant, on the San Pedro River, to help insure that supplies could get through in relative safety.

The men suffered through the winter and apparently looked forward to spring and warmer weather so they could do some farming. But, as a letter from Arizona, dated April 5, 1865, stated, they were to be disappointed. A soldier wrote, "We have planted gardens but the season is more than unusually backward— it snowed yesterday in the mountains. The army worm destroys everything as soon as it comes up, so that chances for raising vegetables are very slim."[85] During the winter of 1864

and the spring and early summer of 1865, the effects of inadequate diet apparently caused more suffering and deaths among troops stationed at Fort Goodwin than the Apaches, thus becoming their primary enemy.

On December 30, 1864, a clemency order issued at Fort Union authorized the officer of the day at Fort Goodwin to release all prisoners in confinement who were serving sentences and return them to duty with their company. The clemency, issued to all New Mexico volunteer troops for the new year of 1865, was accompanied by the "hope that all the men will faithfully do their duty and avoid court-martial."[86]

The incomplete records lack specific details for Company I during the month of January, but without doubt the boring, hard, and sometimes dangerous duty continued as usual with garrison duty, escorts, scouts, and camp building. The two Company I's remained at the post, one of California cavalry volunteers and the other of the New Mexico infantrymen, with Major Gorman continuing as post commander. During January, responsibility for the defense of Arizona Territory was taken away from General Carleton and switched to the Department of the Pacific, headquartered in San Francisco. This action proved both detrimental and discouraging to the commands in the field. Not only were the distances between headquarters and outposts much greater, resulting in long delays from the time orders were issued until they were received, but also the San Francisco headquarters was much less cognizant of true conditions in the area than General Carleton who had marched through it in 1862 and battled Apaches near the site of Fort Bowie.

On February 7, orders show that Captain Simpson was told to detail one of the noncommissioned officers and six privates of Company I to Lieutenant S. R. DeLong, a California volunteer officer, for duty as of 8 a.m. the

63

next day.[87] The orders do not specify what the men would be doing but they would be away from the fort for a considerable time, since they were rationed for 30 days. Perhaps they were going on an Indian scout for it was reported that in early February the Indians committed numerous killings and robberies in southeastern Arizona and attacked the small group of videttes stationed at Fort Buchanan, situated between Tucson and Nogales, Mexico, driving the little party of sentinels out and actually taking control of the post and its equipment.[88]

There was a surprising development at Fort Goodwin in early March. It had been almost 2 months since Major Gorman had sent the Apache emissary back to the chiefs who had proposed peace, but on March 4, the post was electrified by the appearance of 112 Indians, along with three Mexicans, who appeared there under a flag of truce.[89] The party of Indians, which consisted of men, women, and children, held a big pow-wow with Major Gorman. The Indians expressed a strong desire to make a treaty with the post commander but said they wished to return to the mountains and bring in the rest of their families. Major Gorman consented to the request but stipulated that they return in 4 days. The Indians then broke camp and left, but the three Mexicans remained behind at the fort.

When the grace period had passed and the Apaches had not returned, Gorman organized a party of 53 men and left Fort Goodwin at nightfall on March 9.[90] Guided by one of the Mexican captives retained at the fort, Gorman headed for the Indians' rancheria, which the troops reached the second night of their march. Gorman intended to attack the Apaches but the rancheria was deserted because the Indians had been warned of the approach of soldiers by an Apache who had stumbled across their trail. Weather conditions were bad, and melting snow and mud made pursuit of the Apaches difficult, so Gorman gave up and returned his command to the fort.

On March 22, much to the surprise of Major Gorman, a large party of the same Apaches turned up at the fort, again under the protection of a white flag. Gorman and the post returns both put the number at 400, but a personal letter, written from the fort to the *Santa Fe Weekly Gazette,* set the number at 384.[91] Gorman reported a talk with the chiefs, who said they were satisfied they could not fight the white men and all they wanted was some place to plant in peace.[92] The *Santa Fe Gazette* reported that the White Mountain Chief was accompanied by about 180 warriors who could bear arms and that "they were poorly armed, few rifles, very few pistols, and no powder."[93] The report went on to say, "The winter has been very severe and the Indians have suffered greatly. Snow is about four feet deep in the mountains. The Indians say they lost 217 warriors by our scouts last year. They have nothing to eat but mescal...that is a very light diet. Told them about taking them to Bosque (Bosque Redondo Indian reservation). They fear the Navajo, their old enemies."[94]

This mass surrender, exactly the goal for which the troops had been sent to Arizona, now proved an enormous embarrassment. Major Gorman had earlier promised the Indians he would feed and take care of them, with a view toward sending them to the reservation. But a ludicrous turn of events had occurred. With incredibly poor timing, the order, transferring military operations of Arizona Territory to the Department of the Pacific, with headquarters in San Francisco, had arrived the day before the Apaches. This transfer meant that Major Gorman could no longer carry out his promise until he had received authority from his new headquarters.[95] As Gorman put it, "I was placed in the position of the man who drew the elephant in the lottery."[96]

Gorman was in an unenviable spot. He had

400 hungry Indians camped on his doorstep and fewer than 150 troops at the fort because orders for March 12 show that Company I had been told to supply one noncommissioned officer and eight privates to Lieutenant DeLong for another detail for which the men were issued rations for 20 days and 40 rounds of ammunition each.[97] These men, and probably some of the California troops therefore, would have been away from the fort on either escort or scouting duty. It is very probable that other troops were absent as well, since all traffic to and from the post had to be accompanied by armed men through the hazardous countryside. Also, although the Indians were not aware of it, Gorman's own supplies were severely limited, many of his men sick, and his animals in deplorable shape. And the Indians were there as a result of his invitation and promise of help. Gorman pulled a bluff. He later reported, "With nothing to feed them, no transportation to send them to the reservation, and no orders to do so if I had, I made the best of it, and told them they could go until I heard from the great chief."[98] Gorman, with great boldness, even made the chiefs, including the celebrated Es-cut-te-se-la, a White Mountain chief, promise that if any depredations were committed by their people, the Apaches would bring them to the fort and allow Gorman to punish them as he pleased.[99] Apparently the Indians concurred and left the fort, without any trouble, on March 25, to return to the mountains and await word from the post.[100] No word of any deposition of these Indians has been found in the records and even though there were periodic promises of peace from various groups of Indians in the area, depredations continued and the Apaches would be a threat which would not be subdued until the major Apache Wars much later.

On April 9, Company I lost one of its men to what the Army, with unspecific terminology, merely called "disease."[101] At his death, Private

Jose Rafael Apodaca left more numerous effects than the unfortunate Private Romero had. The 30-year-old native of Taos had two of each item of clothing, even bootees, and had also owned a blanket. However, a notation on the Army records stated that all the items were old, worn, and useless.

On April 15, Major Gorman ordered Lieutenant Mann of Company I to take a detachment of 11 privates from the company to escort a train of wagons to the Pima village near Maricopa Wells to the west, and back. He ordered the men to be rationed for 25 days and had each supplied with 40 rounds.[102] Later that month, events of the Civil War, back in the East, were to touch upon the lives of some men at the isolated post situated thousands of miles to the west. On April 24, General Order No. 1 was issued from military headquarters in Santa Fe extending a general amnesty to all military prisoners, regardless of their crimes.[103] The amnesty was issued in honor of the capture of Richmond and Petersburg, Virginia, by the Union Army. The order directed that all prisoners be released and returned to duty, even those who had been sentenced to be drummed out of the service. All those whose pay had been stopped would have it started again, but the men were informed that they would have to make up any time owed and would have to pay any fines they had due.

Records show that in May, Company I supplied one sergeant and seven privates to escort a citizen train, as the civilian commercial merchant trains were called, to Tubac and then back again to the post.[104] The trip to Tubac was about a 257 kilometer (160-mile) journey and the men were rationed for 10 days and issued 40 rounds of ammunition each.

June 11, 1865, marked the death of another private of Company I.[105] Antonio Jose Martin, 24, a native of Abiquiu, was listed only as a victim of "disease" but a contributing factor, if not the major one, was probably dietary

65

deficiencies, as may have been the case in the death of Jose Apodaca, two months earlier. The personal records of Sergeant Charles Hynes also show that he was sick, both in the post hospital and in his quarters, from July through December, 1865.

From shortly after its organization, Company I had had the same men filling the position of first sergeant and the four ranks of sergeant. On June 18 the upper heirarchy of noncommissioned officers experienced a dramatic change. First Sergeant David McAllister, a Kentuckian who had fought at the Battle of Valverde in 1862 as a Regular Army sergeant, was given a discharge for physical disability.[106] He was replaced by Sergeant Jose Eugenio Romero, the man who had been suffering the effects of scurvy. On the same day Sergeant William H. S. Bonsall was reduced in rank to private but no reason for the action is included in his service record.[107] Seven months earlier Bonsall had been made post commissary sergeant for Fort Goodwin. Now, however, Victor Medina was promoted to sergeant in his place and Bonsall served out the remainder of his enlistment as a private. No one was promoted to replace Romero as sergeant, leaving the company without one sergeant for the balance of its existence.

On June 20, Lieutenant Mann and Privates Jose Chaves, Juan de Jesus Cordova, Jose Felipe Martinez, and Gabriel Mata were detailed to escort duty to Tucson.[108] On June 29 there was a flurry of excitement at Fort Goodwin as Governor Goodwin, Brigadier General John Mason, and their staffs, arrived on an inspection trip. The party, escorted by a company of California cavalrymen, was on their way from Fort Bowie to Prescott, Arizona.[109] Mason, the district commander, later reported, "I do not think it (Fort Goodwin) a good post for cavalry, and will, as soon as I can do so, replace the company there by infantry."[110] He was, of course, referring to the California cavalry volunteers who shared the post with Company I. Other changes he made were to relieve the post commander and the surgeon, both of whom he said were not "fitted for their positions, owing to their constant use of intoxicating liquors."[111] On July 5 the inspection party left the post to continue on to Prescott.

Orders issued at Fort Goodwin during July illustrate some of the additional duties carried out by the Company I infantrymen. Orders of July 2 show that Privates Jose Benita Ortiz, Lorenzo Gomez, Rafael Valdez, and Encarnacion Gonzales were detailed to daily duty as teamsters and on July 19, Corporal Jose de Jesus Cascias relieved Sergeant Charles Hynes as corral master of the post.[112]

On July 6, 1865, Corporal Cerdio Mauchago and six privates of Company I were ordered to leave the next morning at 7 a.m. to escort a government wagon "conveying citizens" to Fort Cummings, New Mexico. They were ordered to return "with the transportation to this post without unnecessary delay."[113] Despite their orders to return immediately, when the group arrived at Fort Cummings they were ordered to proceed, on July 17, on to Las Cruces with the government wagons.[114] This they did, returning to Cummings where orders were issued on July 25, telling them to leave the next morning for Fort Bowie, "taking the Mail and 1 Government wagon and 11 Citizens enroute to California."[115] Once they finished the assignment, the men apparently returned the last 193 kilometers (120 miles) to Fort Goodwin. Even though their original orders had been merely to travel to Fort Cummings and return, subsequent orders had required them to cover hundreds more miles and had resulted in their being away from home base for at least a month. Company I could ill afford to have these men away on extended duty for they were seriously under strength and had been in this condition for a considerable length of time.

A normal complement for a New Mexico

volunteer company was between 83 and 100 men, including officers. When Company I arrived at Fort Goodwin, its troop strength was only 77 and by the summer of 1865 it had dropped to an average of 72. Unlike its sister company at Fort Bowie, Company A, I did not appear to be able to supplement its ranks by enlistments. Although I had the full complement of three officers, it had fewer noncoms than most companies, with four sergeants instead of the usual five and five corporals instead of eight. Illness also continued to take its toll, keeping a certain number of men too sick to report for duty on any given day. For example, Lieutenant Felmer was ill with hepatitis from July 10 through July 23 and Sergeant McAllister, a 15-year veteran of military service, was on sick report for 2 months prior to his discharge.[116]

On August 5, Second Lieutenant Joseph Felmer, accompanied by one noncommissioned officer and 10 privates from Company I, was detailed to 9 days' duty away from the post.[117] Shortly after his return, on August 15, a Special Order was issued from Headquarters, District of Arizona, in Prescott, which relieved him from duty at Fort Goodwin and ordered him to report to Headquarters, District of New Mexico in Santa Fe.[118] The same order stated that the post commanders would furnish him with an escort to Fort Bowie and then on to Fort Cummings. Felmer, however, was apparently not released from duty at Fort Goodwin and allowed to leave. Back in May, 1865, General Carleton had recommended to Governor Connelly of New Mexico that Felmer be promoted and appointed first lieutenant of Company D of the volunteers, stationed at Fort Bascom, New Mexico, at the time.[119] On May 11, the headquarters at Santa Fe transmitted the commission, requesting that Felmer be sent to Santa Fe to be mustered in.[120] The order was endorsed, with approval, through the District of Arizona headquarters and there is nothing

in the records to show why Felmer never received the promotion. However, 3 months had passed since inception of the original order and perhaps it was not feasible to release Felmer. At any rate, records show that Felmer remained at Fort Goodwin and the first lieutenant's position in Company D was never filled.

On August 25, Lieutenant Felmer was ordered to take one noncommissioned officer and nine privates of Company I and leave Fort Goodwin the next morning, shortly after sunrise, to escort a government wagon train to Tucson.[121] Felmer apparently never went, or else had to turn back because the distance to Tucson was 193 kilometers (120 miles) and the men were issued 8 days' rations to feed them on their way there. By September 1, only a week after he was to have left, records show that Felmer was listed as sick and under treatment through the 11th of September. The pressure of work was too great, however, to allow any of the men much time to recuperate and by September 17, Felmer was ordered to lead 10 of the Company I men on escort of a government train of wagons to Tucson.[122]

In spite of the attempted surrender of the Apaches at Fort Goodwin the previous spring, most Indians of southeastern Arizona had remained hostile and continued to be a real threat throughout the summer and into the fall of 1865. On August 31, General Mason said that a large band of Indians had been reported on the warpath in one area and others were reported near the San Pedro River and in the vicinity of Fort Bowie at various times from July through October.[123]

November 9 brought about some big changes at Fort Goodwin with the influx of three California volunteer infantry companies, apparently at the behest of General Mason. The California cavalry company, which had served with Company I at Fort Goodwin since the previous August, left and was replaced by 164 men from the three new companies.[124]

Accompanying them was Lieutenant Colonel Robert Pollock who assumed command of Fort Goodwin. With this move, troop strength at the post jumped from the previous 145 to 236.

During the second half of November two Apaches appeared at Fort Goodwin, stating their tribe had a captive child which could be ransomed. Hoping that it was a particular child which had been reported captured by Apaches at a massacre near Pimo Cienega in July, Lieutenant Colonel Pollock ordered Lieutenant Felmer to take a squad of 10 Company I men and accompany the two Indians back to their camp. Felmer left at 10 a.m. and marched about 40 kilometers (25 miles) down the Gila River that day.[125] The next morning, after marching another 16 kilometers (10 miles), he and his men were met by some members of the tribe who led them to their temporary camp, situated in a sandy arroyo about 1.6 kilometers (a mile) from the Gila. Felmer found about 70 Apaches here and talked to their chief, Nom-nel-te-tschigh or "Yellow Hat." The child was not present at the time of their arrival so the soldiers camped there overnight. Felmer later reported that the Indians showed great hospitality, cooking for his men and showing them many attentions. The next morning, when the child was brought to him, Felmer was disappointed to discover that it was not the one he had anticipated. He described the child as "apparently Mexican, about 5 years old, and could talk nothing but a few words of Indian."[126] Felmer, aware that it was impossible for him to comply with the chief's demand for the purchase of the child, and aware that "Yellow Hat" was a friendly chief who had come to Fort Goodwin the previous spring, did not want to cause any controversy. He talked the chief into promising to accompany him back to the fort and, later to bring in his whole band. "Yellow Hat," along with 11 warriors and one squaw, returned to Fort Goodwin with Felmer's detail on November 25.

Friendly Apaches were in the minority in the area, however, and now that Fort Goodwin had additional men to be used on Indian scouts, one was ordered. The day Lieutenant Felmer returned with "Yellow Hat," Captain Simpson, with a large party of men, left to search the country to the north and west "until striking the River San Carlos."[127] Simpson had, under his command, a captain and second lieutenant, four noncommissioned officers and 18 privates—all California volunteers—along with two sergeants, two corporals, and 24 privates from his own Company I. The party was well fitted out with 30 days' rations, all necessary transportation for subsistence supplies, and a variety of medicines, complete with instructions for use, which had been chosen by the post hospital steward as appropriate. The scouting party was warned that "this detachment will not leave the pursuit of Indians for any other purpose unless forced by absolute necessity."[128] No results of the scout were found in the records but the detachment returned after only 17 days in the field, even though they had been rationed for 30.

Four days before Captain Simpson left on the scout another of his men died. Private Juan de Jesus Cordova, 31, who had been a laborer in Taos before his enlistment, died of disease. Some months later Captain Simpson would write a "letter of effects-final statement" in which he listed the items left by Cordova.[129] He would list one shirt, one pair of drawers, one pair of pants, one pair of bootees, a great coat, a pair of stockings, a fatigue hat, a fatigue coat of flannel, and a blanket, and state that all the items were in good condition and used in dressing Cordova for burial.

On December 11, when Captain Simpson returned from the scout, he was faced with some serious unpleasantness. He hardly had time to remove his boots when he learned that six charges had been filed against him with the commanding officer, Lieutenant Colonel

Pollock. The charges, which had been pre-ferred by Mr. C. Whitney, the former sutler at Fort Goodwin, now a private citizen, included such items as conduct unbecoming an offi-cer, irregularities in the disposal of government property, giving whiskey to Indians, keeping his men from paying the sutler in violation of Army regulations, and the violation of two articles of war.[130] The article of war charges stemmed from the alleged disappearance of $220 which had been given to Simpson to be forwarded to the family of one of the men, and his alleged failure to pay the government the salary and allowances for a soldier he was em-ploying as his personal servant.

Part of the antagonism between the sutler and Simpson appeared to begin in early Sep-tember over debts the sutler swore were owed to him by some of the enlisted men in Simpson's company. The sutler charged that the men owed him $2.66 per month for a period of 8 months, or a total of $21.28 each, and he quoted an Act of the 1863 Congress, which set allowances, as his justification.[131] Simpson, on the other hand, was accused of telling his men that they were obliged to pay only $13.00 and that nothing could make them pay more. Apparently the issue became very heated, with tempers flaring on both sides, and Simpson was accused of saying, later in Sep-tember, that he would give the sutler all the trouble he could in collecting his accounts against the troops of the post.

Matters apparently came to a head on Oc-tober 8 when Simpson was acting as president of a board of administration which was con-vened for examination of the sutler's business. Whitney, the sutler, charged that Simpson did "get out of his seat and walk across the tent to where the sutler sat and shake his fist in his face and call him a God damn liar, or words to that effect."[132]

The first witness called at the hearing, which began the very day of Simpson's return

to the fort, was Second Lieutenant Felmer. Felmer stated that he had not seen Simpson playing cards with some Indian women, nor had he seen the captain give them liquor or get them drunk, as had been charged. When ques-tioned about whether Simpson had said he would "bust the sutler up in business," Felmer again answered in the negative.[133] Felmer did admit that he had been aware of the dispute between his commanding officer and the sutler but said he didn't pay any attention to it. Then Felmer was asked whether or not Simpson had said "he would do all in his power to prevent his men from paying the sutler" and the lieutenant replied that Simpson had not uttered those words but had merely said "he could not make his men pay the sutler."[134]

The questioning then shifted to another of the charges. Felmer testified that he had no knowledge of Simpson ever trading or selling government property to the Indians and stated that in his capacity as acting assistant quarter-master of the fort he would be likely to know if any such trading or selling had taken place.

The next witness called was First Lieu-tenant James Mann. When questioned as to whether or not he remembered seeing Captain Simpson talking to some Indian women at the fort the previous summer, Mann admitted that he had and said that the incident had taken place at his quarters. He denied, however, that he had seen his commanding officer playing cards with the women or giving them liquor. He also denied ever having heard Captain Simpson advise his men not to pay the sutler.

The inquiry then moved to another of the allegations, that Captain Simpson had given First Sergeant McAllister, when he received his disability discharge at the post in June, a gov-ernment Springfield musket to take with him when he left. Mann testified that he had seen the sergeant at the captain's quarters just as he was leaving the post and that he did not see him carrying the weapon. He said that, as a matter

69

of fact, Company I was not, and had not been, armed with Springfield muskets.

The next subject Mann was questioned on was his knowledge about an incident in which Sergeant Charles Hynes was reputed to have given Captain Simpson $220 in February to send to his family. Mann testified that the sergeant had told him that he gave the money to Simpson who had, in turn, given it to General Clarke, Surveyor General of the Territory of New Mexico, who presumably was to deliver it in person. One of the specifications in the charges brought against Simpson was that his statement to Hynes about sending the money by General Clarke was false. Sergeant Hynes, however, testified a little later in the hearing that Captain Simpson had mailed the money instead of giving it to Clarke. Mann also testified that Sergeant Hynes told him Captain Simpson had repaid the money to him. Mann's testimony ended with a slight note of exasperation on his part when he was asked whether or not Captain Simpson confided in him about his private business affairs and about whether or not he paid his just debts. Mann, apparently thinking of his long hours on Indian scouts, escort duties, and post chores, answered rather shortly, "No, sir. I have generally as much as I can attend to without meddling in the captain's business."[135]

When Sergeant Hynes was called to testify he stated that when the money disappeared, Captain Simpson gave him a receipt for it, saying he would be responsible. Hynes also testified that Simpson had since repaid him. When questioned about whether he had heard of other cases in which money, sent through the mails, had disappeared, Hynes said that among the California cavalrymen who had been stationed at Fort Goodwin a "heap of fellows sent money to California but never one cent of it was received."[136] He further stated, however, "My captain (Simpson) has sent over $5,000 for different men of our company and never was any money miscarried but this."

After a clerk at the sutler's store, Theophilus Cooper, testified much the same as Lieutenant Felmer and Lieutenant Mann regarding the Indian women, the card playing, and the liquor, the testimony was completed. Surprisingly, one of the charges was totally ignored and no questions were asked about it. The sutler had alleged that Simpson employed one of the soldiers as a servant but had failed to pay the Army paymaster the wages and allowances due for his services, as was the custom in the military at that time. The hearing skirted that issue entirely.

Colonel Pollock forwarded the testimony to the district headquarters in Prescott, stating that this was all the evidence which could be obtained in and about the post, and making no further comment. On November 23, the Assistant Adjutant General at Prescott forwarded the records over an endorsement which said, "These charges seem to have been preferred by a sutler because the officer tried to protect his men from extortion."[137] Apparently the charges were not upheld because Captain Simpson continued on as commander of Company I until its disbandment the next year. Whether or not there was any truth in some of the charges will never be known but, in fact, Captain Simpson appears to have won the battle.

The day after giving his testimony in the proceedings against Captain Simpson, Lieutenant Mann left Fort Goodwin and Company I. The previous August General Carleton had recommended that Mann be promoted to captain and sent to Company A as commanding officer to replace Captain Quintana, who was promoted to major.[138] By November 15, 1865, the recommendation had been approved and made its way through channels to the headquarters of the District of Arizona at Prescott where a Special Order was issued officially relieving Mann of duty at Goodwin.[139] Mann was to be mustered out as a first lieutenant and mustered in as a captain when he arrived at Bowie. He arrived at Fort Bowie on December

15, accompanied by 11 men who had never been mustered in, three of whom had almost served out their time and had never been paid.[140] Apparently it was expected that a mustering officer would be at Fort Bowie to perform the official act necessary to swear the men in, giving them legal status as soldiers. It would seem that the mustering officer was not there and never did appear. Even though Mann took over command of Company A he was not officially mustered in until June, 1866, and his date of rank was then made retroactive to January 1, 1866.

Throughout the winter the daily duties at the outpost continued. On February 14, Sergeant Charles Hynes and six privates from Company I were ordered to escort some sutlers to the Rio Grande and back and were rationed for 20 days.[141] Three of the privates who accompanied Hynes were Jose Pedro Montoya, Jesus Maria Moya, and the former Sergeant William Bonsall. Names of the other three are unknown. Apparently Colonel Pollock, for some reason, felt that Company I might soon depart from Fort Goodwin, for in the orders he issued the men he stated, "If, in returning, this detachment should meet their company en route to New Mexico, the Sergeant in charge shall report to the Company Commander."[142]

On February 20, Private Jose Delores Cruz of Company I was listed as a member of an escort party which left on its way to Fort Bowie. On March 1, Captain Simpson led a large scouting party out from Fort Goodwin accompanied by Lieutenant Felmer, two sergeants, four corporals, and 36 privates of Company I.[143] This was probably all of the company present at the fort at that time who were capable of making the scout. The men were rationed for 20 days but stayed out several days longer. They were ordered to scout the country 96 kilometers (60 miles) up the Gila River, north of there 8 kilometers (5 miles), and then south to Mount Graham. They took pack mules with them to transport the rations but the men were specifi-

cally ordered to carry their own blankets, haversacks, and canteens.

On March 5, seven of the Company I privates, who had remained behind at Fort Goodwin, were sent out on escort duty to Tucson, under command of a California volunteer corporal.[144] Also during March, Fort Goodwin was inspected by Brigadier General Whittier, a special inspector on the staff of the Military Division of the Pacific, who had traveled all the way from the headquarters in San Francisco.[145]

On the last day of the month shocking news reached Fort Goodwin. It was reported that there had been an Indian massacre of United States troops in the neighborhood of Fort Grant, a post situated at the junction of the San Pedro and Aravaipa Rivers, about 64 kilometers (40 miles) southwest of Fort Goodwin. Fort Grant, which was earlier named Fort Breckenridge, was staffed with five companies of men who had marched from Fort Yuma in late October, 1865.[146] The troops were stationed there in an attempt to safeguard the supply route to Fort Goodwin but by December, 1865, post returns stated that the Grant "operations were limited because of a lack of supplies, namely clothing, especially shoes."[147]

Upon receipt of word that there was a problem in the Fort Grant area, Colonel Pollock issued orders that Captain Simpson and Company I, along with a company of the California infantrymen, be prepared to leave Fort Goodwin at reveille on April 1 to scout for Indians in the vicinity of Fort Grant.[148] The men were issued 6 days' rations and took one blanket apiece. They planned to obtain more rations at Grant, enabling them to remain in the area as long as necessary to look for the Indians, but were forced to return to Fort Goodwin on April 11 because of lack of supplies at Fort Grant.[149]

By compiling fragmentary reports from a number of sources, a fairly accurate reconstruction of the massacre can be made. A small

71

party of approximately 12 men, including an escort of nine Regular Army infantrymen, an assistant surgeon of the U.S. Volunteers named Tappan, and an Army paymaster, Brevet Major James Franklin Millar, left Fort Yuma enroute to Fort Grant. Before their departure, Dr. Tappan, somewhat apprehensive of the dangers posed by the Apaches, introduced former-Major John C. Cremony, a veteran of Arizona service, to Major Millar and requested that Cremony give the major some useful information and warnings about traveling the route they were to take. Cremony complied, emphasizing the vigilance necessary even when Apache signs were not evident. The inexperienced Millar rather coolly implied that he was quite capable of managing his own affairs. A few days later, on March 22, 1866, when the party stopped at Cottonwood Springs and broke into small unarmed squads to search for firewood and bring water into camp, they were attacked by Apaches and both Millar and Tappan were killed, along with three other men.[150] Fort Grant post returns show that a detachment from the fort was sent to recover Millar's body. It was found near the springs and buried there. It mentions that an Andrew Snowden died of wounds, the following month, which were received in action near Cottonwood Springs on the same day.[151] Millar was a captain who had been given the brevet promotion to major for gallantry and meritorious service at the Battle of the Wilderness in Virginia in 1864.[152] Cottonwood Springs, a station on the stage road between Yuma and Fort Grant, apparently was a real trouble spot because a wagon master had been killed there several months earlier, in January.[153]

Records do not show that the men from Fort Goodwin made any contact with the hostile Apaches. But apparently this story of a "massacre" became wildly distorted and eventually was reported in leading newspapers on both coasts of the country. The word "massacre" was freely used at the time, and there were almost constant reports of Apache raiding and depredations in Arizona which resulted in a tense and nervous population which freely circulated all kinds of rumors. By May, 1866, while everything was quiet at Fort Goodwin, leading newspapers on the east and west coasts were running stories which stated that Fort Goodwin itself had been overrun by 2,000 Apaches and that 100 soldiers had been massacred with only one trooper living to tell the tale.[154] Publication of such unverified and gory reports was not uncommon in newspapers of the time and later retractions were often printed.

On April 10, Sergeant Hynes and the six privates who had accompanied him to the Rio Grande in February were officially listed as deserters on the Fort Goodwin post returns.[155] Under normal circumstances they should have returned to the post in early March, but they never reappeared. The returns list them as deserting "at or near Las Cruces on or about March 1, 1866, while escorting a train to the Rio Grande."[156] Apparently there was a misunderstanding of some sort. Perhaps the men had expected their company to be marching eastward soon and mentioned it at Fort Selden where, it was decided to retain them. At any rate, they were evidently attached for duty at Fort Selden after their arrival there but this information was not reported back to Captain Simpson at Fort Goodwin. Sergeant Hynes' records show a notation that he was "attached at Fort Selden but not reported" and that he was sick once again and in the hospital at Fort Selden for a period in May and June, 1866. Hynes, who had been a teamster prior to his enlistment at the age of 39, appeared to be a reliable man and unlikely to desert. Private Bonsall's records show that he was given a leave of absence by the commanding officer of Fort Selden in April in order to travel all the way to Fort Craig, New Mexico, to visit his family. Colonel Francisco Abreu, commanding officer of the New Mexico regiment of volunteer infantrymen, wrote a letter from his headquarters at Fort Craig saying that Bonsall had been attached to Company E at the fort, expecting the arrival of Company I there and that Abreu had ordered him, on July 16, to return to Fort Selden in the company of seven New Mexico cavalrymen who were returning to that post. Abreu wrote, "I understood that he has been reported a deserter but he is not." Apparently all the men who had been accused of desertion rejoined Company I on June 21 when it arrived at Fort Selden after leaving Arizona, with the exception of Bonsall, who didn't arrive there until July 19.

While Sergeant Hynes and his men were at Fort Selden expecting Company I to arrive at any time, Captain Simpson's men were continuing their usual chores back at Fort Goodwin. On April 15, two teams of wagons were sent to Fort Bowie to obtain some grain and bring it back to Goodwin.[157] Corporal Jose Manuel Aragon, the man who had requested a transfer to I in order to serve with his father and brother, was put in charge of the escort and assigned six privates to accompany him. Fort Goodwin post returns state that the party returned to Goodwin on April 23. It seems unlikely that the men could have made the trip to Bowie, loaded the wagons, and returned in 9 days if the distance to Bowie was 193 kilometers (120 miles) as is listed in the Fort Goodwin post returns. This would have been a 386 kilometer (240-mile) round trip by the route which was used in those days, requiring the covering of 48 kilometers (30 miles) a day in the lumbering wagons drawn by mules, if a one-day layover at Bowie was allowed for rest and loading the wagons. Present day maps show the distance to be between 128 and 144 kilometers (80 and 90 miles) on roads now in existence and even though, by 1866, the trail between Goodwin and Bowie had been in use for almost 2 years, it is hard to believe grain wagons could have covered so much ground in so little time.

Duty at Fort Goodwin consisted of many humdrum daily jobs in addition to searches for Indians and long trips as escorts away from the post. The men worked as teamsters and herders, carpenters and blacksmiths, built and improved structures at the fort, stood guard duty, cooked, cut firewood, hauled water, and did all the hard and unexciting chores required to make any military post operative. Daily routine began with reveille at 5 a.m., followed by fatigue call at 5:30 and surgeon's call at 6:30 for those who needed medical attention. The soldiers had breakfast at 7:15, fatigue call at 8 a.m. and by 9 there was a guard mounting. At 11:30 a.m. there was a recall from the 8 a.m. fatigue and an orderly call at noon. At 1 p.m. the men ate dinner and they returned to work at 2, finishing at 5 in the afternoon. Retreat was sounded at sunset and by 9 p.m. the sound of the bugle signaled tattoo. By 9:30 taps was sounded and the men bedded down. Every Sunday an inspection was held at 9:30 in the morning.[158]

For several months that spring, the men of Company I had been aware that their tour of duty in Arizona was coming to a close and they would soon be returning to their native New Mexico, eventually to be discharged and once more see their homes and families. The Civil War in the East had finally ended, releasing a number of Federal troops for service in the West. These troops would be used to replace the volunteers who had been so magnificent in protecting the area when regular troops could not. For months rumors had flown about Fort Goodwin, but it was not until early May, 1866, that units of the 14th United States Infantry arrived to take over the post. The volunteers did not leave immediately and for a short transitional period both groups of soldiers were at the fort. Business went on as usual with Lieutenant Felmer and a detail of four Company I men being detailed to detached service on May 9.[159] Orders do not specify what duty they were assigned but they were furnished with a six-mule team and wagon, warned to be properly armed, and rationed for 10 days.

73

On May 10, the new post commander, Major Chapin of the 14th U.S. Infantry, issued an order instituting a new procedure for changing of the guard. It stated that the old guard would "discharge their pieces at the target immediately on being relieved. The name of the soldier who makes the best shot to be entered on the Guard Report."[160] To avoid any frivolous waste of ammunition, Chapin ordered that the Officer of the Day would have the old bullets collected and the lead turned in to the ordnance officer who would place it in the magazine.

The volunteers, veterans of almost 2 years of difficult and hazardous duty at the fort they helped build in the wilderness, must have been amazed at the new orders now being issued from the post commander, orders which pointed out how much more civilized and better supplied the fort had become. Now the mail was to go out weekly for Fort Bowie every Sunday morning and an order listed prices for goods and services which had been settled upon by the council of administration at the post. Some of the items are listed below, and show that some of the Regular Army soldiers would enjoy the luxury of having their families with them.

Price of bread at
Post bakehouse ....20¢ per ration
Pay of Post baker ....30¢ per day
Price of soldier's
washing ....$1.00 per month
Price of officer's
washing (single officer) ...$2.50 per month
Family of 2 ....$3.50 per month
Family of 4 ....$5.00 per month
Family of 6 ....$7.00 per month
    The officer furnishing the soap
    and starch
Price of half soling and heeling shoes ...50¢
Price of patching shoes ....20¢
    The government furnishing the tools
    and leather.[161]

On May 18, the long-awaited order was issued stating that Company I, First Infantry, New Mexico Volunteers, would be held in readiness to proceed to the District of New Mexico to be mustered out of the service.[162] The men from Taos collected their meager belongings and prepared their equipment to move out. Although some of them were ill, and all worn down by poor diet and hardships of their 2 years' duty in Arizona, there must have been high anticipation of a return to their home territory and their loved ones. Two days later, on May 20, Company I was officially released from duty and the decimated company, which now consisted of only two officers and 61 men, began its last long march toward New Mexico.[163]

It is very interesting that no documentation has been found to show that any man from either of the two New Mexico companies was ever killed by Apaches while stationed in Arizona. This is most significant since the California volunteers, doing simultaneous duty in the same area, were often attacked and a number of them slain. Possibly the Indians, who had a long association with both Mexicans and Mexican-Americans, considered them more dangerous enemies and more competent soldiers in the rugged terrain, and avoided them.

By June 1, Company I had arrived at Fort Cummings, New Mexico, after a 12-day march.[164] Lieutenant Felmer, apparently still hoping to receive the promotion he was supposed to have gotten the previous August, left Fort Cummings immediately for Fort Selden but the rest of the company remained at Fort Cummings until June 19, and then marched eastward once again, headed toward Fort Selden on the Rio Grande.[165] Felmer arrived on June 5 and immediately sent off a letter to the headquarters in Santa Fe, citing the order of August 15, 1865, which had ordered him returned to be commissioned a first lieutenant.[166] In the letter Felmer requested further orders. Circumstances, however, apparently worked against him, and he was eventually discharged in Albuquerque, about the same time as the other men, and still a second lieutenant. At the time of his discharge he had seen continuous military service for 5 years and 1 month.

When Company I arrived at Fort Selden it received the disappointing news that a special order had been issued in Santa Fe requiring it to take post at Fort Selden rather than travel on up the Rio Grande toward home.[167] It was to replace Company F of the volunteers, which was ordered to proceed to Fort McRae to be stationed there. This change in plans occurred because some Apaches had murdered some white men in the Pinos Altos area a short time before. As a result, Carleton's Santa Fe headquarters had ordered an Indian scout in an attempt to capture and punish the Indians. A number of troops were ordered out on the search but others, like Company I, were needed to garrison the various posts in the area to safeguard them and carry on routine duties.

Company I arrived at Selden on June 20 and the next day three of the company's privates were detailed as a guard for the government ferry boat which crossed the Rio Grande at the post and one of the noncommissioned officers and four of the privates were ordered to escort a government train to Fort McRae and back.[168]

On July 5, Private Rafael Valdez of Company I was murdered at Fort Selden, shot by someone wielding a pistol in a brawl at the post. The 31-year-old native of Taos, one of the tallest men in the company at 177.5 centimeters (5 feet, 11 inches), had survived all the dangers of duty against the Apaches of Arizona only to die a few months before he was to be discharged.

While Company I was stationed at Fort Selden the men were kept busy with escort duties and even Indian scouts. On July 17, orders were issued detailing one noncommissioned officer and three privates from the company to escort the United States mail to Fort Cummings.[169] The men were instructed to

rest for 24 hours there and then return to Selden "without delay." Lieutenant Felmer was given medical treatment for a severe contusion from July 18 through July 20, but records do not divulge the circumstances under which he was injured. Two days later, however, he was apparently well enough to be ordered out on an Indian scout. The scouting party, commanded by a California cavalry volunteer captain, consisted of 10 enlisted men from Company I, five men from the California cavalry, and three men from a New Mexico volunteer cavalry company.[170] The party was ordered to proceed to the San Diego crossing of the Rio Grande, situated near the San Diego mountain about 16 kilometers (10 miles) southeast of present-day Hatch, New Mexico. From that point the cavalrymen were to "scout the river to the point of the Luna Caballo" to ascertain if any Indians with stock had passed the river. If no signs of Indians were found, they were ordered to wait in the area for a reasonable amount of time to try to intercept any Indian parties that might try to pass.

On July 28, one noncom and three privates from I were ordered on a short trip to escort a government train to Picacho, a stopping place on the Butterfield Trail 9.6 kilometers (6 miles) northwest of Las Cruces.[171] On July 30, another noncommissioned officer, along with four privates of Company I, left the fort to escort a government wagon train to Franklin, Texas, which today is known as El Paso.[172]

On August 1, 1866, Corporal Aragon took five Company I privates and led an escort for a contractor's train headed for Fort Cummings, rationed for 5 days.[173] Shortly after their return to Fort Selden, orders arrived saying that Company I was to leave the post and resume its march toward Albuquerque and eventual discharge. The men left Fort Selden on August 11 and arrived in Albuquerque on August 24, after a march of 344 kilometers (215 miles).[174]

Company I had been operating with only

two officers, Captain Simpson and Second Lieutenant Felmer, ever since the previous December when First Lieutenant Mann had left to become commanding officer of Company A. At the time of Mann's transfer, the headquarters in Santa Fe had ordered that a second lieutenant then serving at Fort Bowie, Thomas Coghlan, be promoted and transferred to Company I to fill the vacancy. Coghlan, like Felmer, could not find a mustering officer to officially make him a first lieutenant nor did he manage to be released to transfer to Goodwin. He, like Felmer, continued to try, for many months, to achieve his goal and, unlike Felmer, was finally successful. In what amounted to little more than a "paperwork exercise," Lieutenant Coghlan transferred to Company I on August 8, 1866, while the two companies were marching north toward Albuquerque separately and, as a matter of fact, Coghlan did not actually join with Company I until both groups were in Albuquerque. Coghlan had apparently found a mustering officer at either Fort Selden or Fort Craig while marching northward with Company A and his commission was made retroactive to January 25, 1866, insuring that he would receive first lieutenant's pay from that period.

Company I remained at the military post at Albuquerque for about 5 weeks preparing for its disbandment. Company F of the volunteers, which had been stationed at Fort Selden, was also there preparing for discharge and soon Company A arrived. The post at Albuquerque must have been a scene of confusing activity as records were scanned to determine which men would be retained in the military and transferred to the newly organized Battalion of New Mexico Volunteers to serve in Colorado against the Utes, and financial records were reviewed to assure that men received back pay or were docked for outstanding debts. Mustering out documents also had to be prepared and arrangements made for men to either turn

in their weapons or purchase them if they desired.

During August and September, eight enlisted men from Company I were retained in the service and officially transferred to the Battalion of New Mexico Volunteers for further duty. Lieutenant Coghlan, who had indicated that he desired to remain in the service, took the enlisted men and marched them to Fort Union, where they joined with other members of the battalion.

On September 18, Lieutenant Felmer was discharged and on September 26, the rest of the members of Company I were released from military service and allowed to make their way home. Captain Simpson returned to Taos and in October of the following year he married Josefa Valdez, a member of one of the oldest Taos families.[175] Josefa was later described by one of her daughters as "very tiny, with big, coal-black eloquent eyes, black silky hair, a perfect lady of dignity."[176] Seven children resulted from the union which lasted for 40 years until the death of Josefa in 1907. At the time of his marriage, Simpson purchased an adobe home southwest of the town plaza on what is today Ledoux Street. The home is now part of a community cultural center housing a public library and art gallery and is called the Harwood Foundation. Tenants and guests at the Harwood Foundation are reputed to have encountered Simpson's ghost, the most recent incident having taken place about 10 years ago.[177] In one such incident, he was supposed to have appeared in knickers and military tunic, saying, "I just thought you should know I was here," and then disappeared through the wall.[178]

Even discounting the ghost stories, the fact remains that Captain Simpson is, and was, a well-known personage in Taos. Prior to his military service he was renown as a friend of Kit Carson, Tom Boggs, Tom Tobin and many other famous trappers and mountaineers with whom he took part in Indian forays, scouted,

Smith Simpson, c. 1900

Author's collection

*Simpson at "Kit" Carson's grave
in Taos*

Courtesy of Kit Carson Museum
Taos, New Mexico

*Oil painting made of Smith Simpson
after his return to civilian life*

Courtesy of Kit Carson Museum
Taos, New Mexico

hunted and camped.[179] The famous flag-pole incident of 1861, in which Simpson took a group of men into Taos Canyon, selected a tall, slender cottonwood, cut it down, trimmed off its branches, and brought it back to the Taos plaza where he, Kit Carson, Ceran St. Vrain and others nailed an American flag to it to raise aloft, had already made him a local celebrity before he raised Company I. The flag, flying night and day over the plaza would insure that Simpson would be remembered, even today, in Taos. As he said, some 50 years after the incident, and shortly before his death, "I am the only one left, but the flag is still there."[180]

After his return from service in Arizona, Simpson farmed the 64 hectares (160 acres) of bounty land he had obtained as a result of his service as a sergeant in the Indian War of 1855 under Colonel Ceran St. Vrain and was known as a "sober, steady citizen" in the words of one of his neighbors.[181] Two years after his return to Taos Simpson was elected representative in the House of the New Mexico Legislative Assembly of 1868.[182] He not only raised stock and farmed but made lengthy travels on horseback through the state on land, lease, title, abstract and claim business. Apparently Simpson suffered after-effects from the wound he alleged he received in his left ankle while on duty in Arizona. In sworn statements, made years later when he was applying for a veteran's pension, he and other witnesses swore that the injury to his Achilles' tendon had caused sciatica, partial paralysis, and a loss of sensation in his left leg and foot. Simpson died in Taos on April 4, 1916, less than a month before his 83rd birthday.

Pension records reveal that some of the Company I men lived in Las Animas county, Colorado, after their return from the service, including Jose Eugenio Romero who had been first sergeant, Corporal Manuel Aragon, Corporal Reyes Duran, and Privates Encarnacion Marruha (Marufo), Antinacia Ribera (Atanacio Rivera), and Jose Marino Lobato (Jose Mariano Lovato).[183] In their pension claims, several of the men blamed long-standing health problems such as rheumatism and digestive disorders on the conditions under which they had been forced to serve in Arizona.

Lieutenant Felmer, shortly after his discharge, returned to Arizona and the scene of his military service. Felmer married an Apache woman and by 1870 was living on a small ranch in the fertile bottomlands of the San Pedro River about 4.8 kilometers (3 miles) above Fort Grant. He was the post blacksmith and also sold vegetables and barley which he raised in his truck garden, to the garrison. During the next several years Felmer became a well-known civilian Indian Scout in that area of Arizona, frequently guiding parties of soldiers in forays against the Apaches as part of General George Crook's Apache campaign.[184] Some years later, in 1898, when he was 69, Felmer was living in Globe, Arizona, just a few miles north of the site of the Pinal Creek Expedition where Company I had fought the Apaches. Felmer's pension records show that he suffered a cerebral hemorrhage in 1900, was taken to the military hospital at Fort Huachuca, Arizona, and later transferred to the Soldiers Home in Los Angeles, California, where he died in 1904 at the age of 75.

Sergeant David McAllister, given a disability discharge at Fort Goodwin, was originally from Kentucky but eventually settled down in Texas. McAllister had been a professional soldier who, before his enlistment in Company I, had received a battlefield commission at the Battle of Valverde but was later forced to resign it. In 1871, at the age of 40, he married a 17-year-old girl in Texas and became a school teacher. He died in 1892, at the age of 61, 42 days before the last of his seven children was born. His widow received a small government pension based on his status as a veteran of the Indian Wars.

Jose de Jesus Cascias (Casias) returned to Taos after his discharge and 10 years later, on September 17, 1877, was shot to death in nearby Elizabethtown, a copper- and gold-mining camp. In testimony for a pension claim, given by Jose Delores Cruz and witnessed by Smith Simpson, Cruz swore that Casias had married Isabella Valencia, a laundress for the company, in June, 1866, prior to his discharge while the company was at Fort Selden. Cruz said, "I was present and witnessed the ceremony and I and my wife were married at the same time. It was a double marriage." Apparently the Casiases also desired to be married in the Church, for records show they were married by the priest in Taos in November, 1866.

So the men of Company I scattered after their disbandment, returning to homes and civilian occupations, many marrying and starting families. As the years passed, memory of hardships endured in Arizona probably faded, although some were undoubtedly reminded by physical ailments which had had their beginnings in the exposure and poor diet of those earlier days. Perhaps a few even conjectured, on occasions, as to what had been accomplished by their labors as news reports continued to come from Arizona until the 1880s about Apache raids and killings. Later events were certainly to prove King Woolsey wrong when he wrote, in 1864 shortly after the Pinal Creek Expedition, "We have followed the trail of the Apache to his home in the mountains, and have learned where it is located; we have dispelled the idea of vast numbers that has ever been attached to that tribe. A few hundred of poor miserable wretches compose the formidable foe as much dreaded by many. They will be brought to terms easily or exterminated, I cannot doubt, when once the Government shall know how small is the enemy by which so much annoyance has been caused."[185]

General Carleton, too, in the first flush of his enthusiasm in mounting his Apache Exped-

ition, certainly expected to make a quick job of disposing of the Apache threat. He planned a preliminary thrust to last approximately 60 days during which all the military units at his disposal in the area would have all possible troops out in the field at the same time the civilian miners and friendly Indians he had armed were also scouting. He obviously hoped this sudden military activity, carried on at the same time at a number of points, would confuse and rout the Indians and give them the impression of more troops than he actually had. As Carleton himself said, "This covering of so much ground by detachments of determined men moving simultaneously from so many different points, *must* produce a moral effect upon the Indians which it is hoped will convince them of the folly long to hold out against us."[186]

Unfortunately, Carleton's plans did not materialize as he had envisioned them. Apparently he misjudged the logistics of a quick and effective campaign against Arizona Apaches. Possibly his earlier successes against Navajos and Mescalero Apaches of southern New Mexico had made him underestimate the Apaches of Arizona, who were considered by many to be the wiliest, bravest, and most fierce of the white men's enemies in the West.

Problems for the Apache Expedition arose almost from the beginning. The two New Mexico companies did not arrive in Las Cruces in time to move westward with the central force and had to straggle in later. Even when Fort Goodwin was established, more than a month after the first units left Las Cruces, it was only a rudimentary facility of brush houses and tents and the supply lines necessary to provide food and equipment for the troops were very extended and passed through much rugged and hazardous country, with the result that they were often left underprovisioned. Some supplies were sent from New Mexico, some arrived via mule team caravans from California, and others were sent by ship to Guaymas, Sonora, Mexico, and then transported northward to Tubac, Arizona Territory.[187]

Carleton may well have underrated the Apache abilities to operate in the harsh countryside and their determination to avoid capture. The Indians, apparently, were well aware, most of the time, of the number of troops out in the field and their location. Captain Shaw, the New Mexico cavalryman, continually discovered deserted rancherias on his scout down toward Fort Goodwin in 1864 and stated on one occasion, "All the rancherias are deserted, the women and children doubtless hidden in the fastness of these mountain gorges."[188] On another occasion, the Apaches he met told him they had been aware of his approach for several days. On the 26th of June, a Mexican woman who had, for years, been a captive of the Apaches and had just escaped, came into his camp. She told him the Indians he had been hunting had left the area and gone over to the Gila River. Shaw wrote, "She also stated that the Indians...had constantly watched my movements since the 8th of June, and when they found that I was returning they had with their families continued to dodge me and finally to get around me, and had escaped, and did not intend to return to their old haunts whilst my command had remained in the mountains."[189]

The Apaches, totally knowledgeable about their home territory, were adept at avoiding scouting parties and indulged in "hit and run" tactics against small groups of soldiers and travelers rather than any large confrontations.

It did not take long for the men actually involved in the field operations against the Apaches to become aware of the futility in trying to defeat the Indians with the limited military manpower available. Captain Shaw, whose scouting party consisted of 63 men, wrote, at the end of his 51-day scout, that he estimated the warriors of the Sierra Blanca and vicinity numbered between 350 and 400.[190] Shaw stated that the Sierra Blanca Apaches "have the reputation of fighting troops man for man" and he felt that, "owing to the nature of the country a force of less than 125 to 150 (would be) inadequate to prosecute successfully a war against them, simply because a less number cannot cover simultaneously enough ground."[191] Some months later, in April, 1865, Major Gorman wrote from Fort Goodwin, "...hunting them (the Apaches) over this immense Territory with only six companies is simply an absurdity."[192]

So it would appear that a combination of factors prevented the Apache Expedition from being a success. Carleton had insufficient troops on hand to begin with and this number was further reduced by necessity to utilize many of them to escort every traveler, every supply train, every messenger, and every mail carrier dispatched between points in the territory. Illness took a far worse toll among the troops than the Indians with fevers, dysentery, scurvy, and sundry ailments caused by exposure, bad water, and inadequate diets. The Indians' determination to avoid capture and reject the throught of surrender had been heightened by rumors that Navajo men, who had been rounded up earlier, had all been killed by their captors.

When the first few months of military activity in Arizona failed to achieve Carleton's aim of rapid subjugation of the Apaches, the whole situation changed. By mid-1865, a number of the California volunteer troops left the area to be mustered out and the main duty of the few remaining soldiers became a sort of holding action whereby they garrisoned the posts and safeguarded travel routes. When the two New Mexico companies completed their service in Arizona, the Apaches were still unconquered.

History would not remember the men of Company I as heros, in fact, it would hardly remember them at all. They fought no great battles and changed the course of events very little. Even Fort Goodwin, which they so laboriously helped build, would be abandoned by the Army in 1871, after almost every soldier and family was hit by fever in 1870.[193] But the volunteers carried out their duties as ordered. They marched the weary miles in all kinds of weather, bedded down on inhospitable ground with their one blanket, chased Apaches, and safeguarded the supply trains while often suffering from loneliness, sickness, and isolation. They were good soldiers and that, after all, is one of the highest accolades that can be given them.

81

ADDENDUM

General Information on Company I Personnel

Place of Birth:

Mexico	3
New York	2
Kentucky	1
Scotland	1
Italy	1
Germany	1
New Mexico	70
(Taos	42)
Unknown	18

Average Height: 5'3" to 5'6"

Average Age: Born between 1833 and 1843

Deserted: 16 men

Died: 7 men

Disabled: 2 men

Ethnic Make-up of Company: 97 total
   10 Anglo
   87 Spanish

	Total	Anglo	Spanish
Officers	5	5	0
1st Sgt.	2	1	1
Sgt.	5	2	3
Cpl.	11	1	10
Pvt.	90	3	87

NOTE: Figures above reflect the fact that some enlisted men held several ranks.

DIED

Name	Date	Location	Cause
Pvt. Jose Rafael Apodaca	April 9, 1865	Ft. Goodwin, A.T.	Disease
Pvt. Juan de Jesus Cordova	Nov. 25, 1865	Ft. Goodwin, A.T.	Disease
Pvt. Antonio Jose Martin	June 11, 1865	Ft. Goodwin, A.T.	Disease
Pvt. Antonio Meistes	Dec. 29, 1864	Ft. Goodwin, A.T.	Disease (Scurvy)
Pvt. Mileton Ocania	June 3, 1864	Ft. Union, N.M.	Tuberculosis
Pvt. Felipe Romero	Aug. 19, 1864	Ft. Goodwin, A.T.	Disease
Pvt. Rafael Valdez	July 5, 1866	Ft. Selden, N.M.	Shot in brawl

DISABLED

Name	Date	Location	Cause
2nd Lt. Edward E. Ayer	May 31, 1864	Ft. Craig, N.M.	Deformed foot
1st Sgt. David McAllister	June 18, 1865	Ft. Goodwin, A.T.	Rheumatism

DESERTED

84

Sixteen men, out of a total of 97, deserted from Company I, which is a 16% desertion rate. This was a very low desertion rate and none of the men deserted after they reached their permanent duty station, Fort Goodwin.

Name	Date	Location
Pvt. Pedro Archuleta	Dec. 21, 1863	Ft. Union, N.M.

(Caught Sept. 4, 1865 at Golandrinas, N.M. Sentenced to serve time with ball and chain and shaved head and then be drummed out. Discharged, instead, several months later.

Pvt. Juan Antonio Baco	Jan. 18, 1864	Ft. Union, N.M.
Pvt. Jose Antonio Bueno	April 11, 1864	Ft. Union, N.M.
Pvt. Juan Jose Cordova	Jan. 3, 1864	Ft. Union, N.M.
Pvt. Jose Rafael Cruz	May 26, 1864	Luis Lopez, N.M.
Pvt. Jose D. Espinosa	April 11, 1864	Ft. Union, N.M.

(Joined to duty, September 16, 1864, in confinement until transferred to Company G, Feb. 1, 1865.)

Cpl. Peter Frank	May 8, 1864	Las Vegas, N.M.
Cpl. Juan de los Reyes Gonzales	May 8, 1864	Las Vegas, N.M.
Pvt. Pedro Lopez	Dec. 18, 1863	Enroute to Sante Fe, N.M.
Pvt. Juan Domingo Martin	Jan. 20, 1864	Ft. Union, N.M.

(After desertion, joined Company K on Feb 29, 1864, discovered and returned to I on May 1, 1864, served honorably until Sept., 1866, then trans. to Bttn. of N.M. Vols.)

Pvt. Jose Mestes	April 24, 1864	Ft. Union, N.M.
Pvt. Inierino Montoya	Feb. 22, 1864	Ft. Union, N.M.

(Caught, returned to duty, served until Sept. 1866, then trans. to Bttn. of N.M. Vols.)

Pvt. Juan Rivelle	April 11, 1864	Ft. Union, N.M.
Pvt. Jose Ignacio Sanches	Feb. 20, 1864	Ft. Union, N.M.
Pvt. Francisca Unopa	Dec. 12, 1863	Taos, N.M.
Pvt. Jose Antonio Valdes	May 11, 1864	Rio Pecos, N.M.

PRIOR MILITARY SERVICE

Listed below is information which was discovered about prior military service of members of Company I. It should be kept in mind that the listing is undoubtedly incomplete and the exclusion of a man's name is no proof he had not seen earlier service.

2nd Lt. Edward E. Ayer—Sgt., Company E, 1st Cavalry, California Vols.

Pvt. Jose de Jesus Cascias (Casias)—Served in Capt. Mink's Independent Spy Co., 1861–1862

Cpl. Juan de los Reyes Duran—New Mexico Mounted Vols., Ute Indian Wars, Jan. to June, 1855. Also, Third New Mexico Mounted Vols., Sept. 1861–May 1862 (Bugler)

2nd Lt. Joseph Felmer—Sgt., Company C, California Cavalry Vols. August 1861 to June 1864

1st Lt. James Mann—Company F., U.S. Infantry, served 6 years. Member of Utah Expedition, Navajo Expedition, and fought at Battle of Valverde.

Pvt. George Martin—Records list as veteran soldier but give no particulars. Martin was born in Scotland in 1828.

1st Sgt. David McAllister—Sgt., Mounted Rifles and 3rd Cavalry, U.S. Army, August 1851 to May 1862. Also, First Cavalry, New Mexico Vols., May 1862 to Dec. 1863. Battlefield promotion to 2nd Lt. at Valverde, later promoted to 1st Lt., resigned, Dec. 1863.

1st Sgt. Jose Eugenio Romero—1st Sgt., Company D, 3rd Infantry, New Mexico Mounted Vols., August 1861 to March 1862

Capt. Smith Simpson—Sgt., Company C, Battalion of New Mexico Mounted Vols., Ute Indian War, Jan. to July, 1855. Wounded in the leg.

Above information from Individual Service Records and Pension Records, NA.

85

COMPANY I
ROSTER

Listed below is a roster of the men in Company I. Maximum authorized strength for a New Mexico Volunteer Infantry Company was: 1 Captain, 1 First Lieutenant, 1 Second Lieutenant, 1 First Sergeant, 4 Sergeants, 8 Corporals, 2 Musicians, 1 Wagoner, and from 64 to 82 Privates. Companies, however, were seldom up to full strength.

In the list below, a soldier's name can be listed more than once if he was promoted, i.e., once as a private and again as a corporal, for the roster shows the names of those who served at each rank during the life of the company. Innumerable inaccuracies in the spelling of Spanish names were found, however, all names are listed in the roster as they appear on the official records. In cases where the correct spelling was determined from another source, it is included in parenthesis.

CAPTAIN

SIMPSON, Smith H.

87

1ST LIEUTENANT

COGHLAN, Thomas

MANN, James

2ND LIEUTENANT

AYER, Edward E.

FELMER, Joseph

1ST SERGEANT

McALLISTER, David

ROMERO, Jose Eugenio

SERGEANT

BARELA, Ramon
BONSALL, William H. S.
HYNES, Charles

MEDINA, Victor
ROMERO, Jose Eugenio

CORPORAL

ARAJON, Manuel (Aragon)
CASCIAS, Jose de Jesus (Casias)
DURAN, Reyes
FRANK, Peter
GONZALES, Juan de los Reyes
LOBATO, Jose Marino (Lovato, J. Mariano)

MAUCHAGO, Cerdio
MEDINA, Victor
MESTES, Juan Esidorio
ROMERO, Antonia Ma
SILVA, Juan Nepomocina

PRIVATE

ABILA, Juan de Jesus

APODACA, Jose Rafael

ARAGON, Pedro Antonio

ARAJON, Manuel (Aragon)

ARCHULETA, Pedro

ARGUELLA, Fernandes

ARRAGON, Jesus (Aragon)

BACA, Juan

BACO, Juan Antonio

BARELA, Ramon

BONSALL, William H. S.

BUENO, Jose Antonio

BUENO, Matteo

CANDELARIO, Jesus

CASADOS, Jose Maria

CASCIAS, Jose de Jesus (Casias)

CHAVEZ, Jose

CHERINO, Felis

COCA, Vicente

CORDOVA, Juan de Jesus

CORDOVA, Juan Jose

CRUZ, Felipe

CRUZ, Jose Delores

CRUZ, Jose Felipe

CRUZ, Jose Rafael

DOMINGUES, Delfedos

ESPINOSA, Jose D.

ESPINOSA, Jesus Maria

FRANK, Peter

GOMEZ, Lorenzo

GONZALES, Encainacion (Encarnacion)

GONZALES, Jose Francisco

GONZALES, Juan de los Reyes

GONZALES, Juan Jose

GONZALES, Loretto

GRIEGO, Manuel Jose

GURALIA, Jose

GURALIE, Jose Cusinoro

HYNES, Charles

LOBATO, Jose Marino (Lovato, J. Mariano)

LOPEZ, Pedro

LUJAN, Christobal

MADENO, Jose Jesus

MARRUHA, Jose Encarnacion (Marufo)

MARTIN, Antonio Jose

MARTIN, George

MARTIN, Geronemo

MARTIN, Jose Manuel

MARTIN, Juan Domingo

MARTINEZ, Jose Felipe

MATA, Gabriel P.

MAUCHAGO, Cerdio

MEDINA, Jose Mateo

MEDINA, Juan Pomaceno

MEDINA, Victor

MEISTES, Antonio (Mestes)

MESTES, Jose

MESTES, Juan Esidorio

MONTONYO, Georges

MONTOYA, Inierino

MONTOYA, Jose Margarito

MONTOYA, Jose Pedro

MOYA, Jesus Maria

NEBRETA, Bartola

OCANIA, Mileton

ORTEGA, Caterino

ORTEZ, Ramon

ORTIZ, Jose Benita

RIBERA, Antinacia (Rivera, Atanacio)

RIBERA, Gabriel

RIVELLE, Juan

88

RODRIEGEZ, Jose Rafael
RODRIGUES, Anastacio
ROMERO, Antonio Ma
ROMERO, Dioniceo
ROMERO, Felipe
ROMERO, Jose Eugenio
ROMERO, Juan Jose

SALAZAR, Jose
SANDOVAL, Juan

SANCHES, Jose Ignacio
SILVA, Juan Nepomocina
SUASO, Rafael

TAFFOYA, Nestor

UNOPA, Francisco
URBAN, Manuel

VALDES, Jose Antonio
VALDEZ, Rafael

MUSICIAN

MARQUES, Ramon

SERVENA, Cosma

LAUNDRESS

VALENCIA, Isabella

90

FOOTNOTES

NOTE: To avoid repetitive listings of long-titled National Archives microfilmed sources, each of these sources has been assigned a reference number and will be identified here at the beginning of the footnotes. Other sources are footnoted in the conventional manner.

Source #1—Record Group 94, Records of the Adjutant General, "Post Returns of Fort Cummings, N.M., 1863–1873."

Source #2—Record Group 98, "Post Orders, Fort Cummings, N.M., 1863–1873."

Source #3—Record Group 94, Returns from U.S. Military Post, Fort Grant, Ariz., Oct. 1865–Dec. 1874, Microcopy 617, Roll 414.

Source #4—Record Group 393, Records of U.S. Army Continental Command, 1821–1920, Fort Selden, N.M., "Letters Sent," Vol. 7A-1866, pp. 1–49.

Source #5—Record Group 393, Records of U.S. Army Continental Command, 1821–1920, Fort Selden, N.M., "General and Special Orders," Vols. 23A and 23B.

Source #6—Record Group 94, Returns from U.S. Military Post, Albuquerque, N.M., Oct. 1846–July 1867, Microcopy 617, Roll 13.

Source #7—Record Group 94, Records of the Adjutant Generals Office, 1783–1917, Regimental Record Book, Civil War, 1st Reg., N.M. Infantry, "Letters Sent and Received and Orders, 1861–1866."

Source #8—Record Group 94, Compiled Service Records of Volunteer Union Soldiers who served in Organizations from the Territory of New Mexico, Microcopy 427.

Source #9—Record Group 94, Records of the Adjutant Generals Office, "Post Returns from U.S. Military Post, 1800–1916," Fort Goodwin, A. T., Microcopy 617.

Source #10—Pension Records, Individual Soldiers, National Archives, Washington, D.C.

91

1. Individual Muster Roll of Smith H. Simpson, Source #8. *NOTE: Hereafter, information gleaned from Individual Muster Rolls will not always be footnoted. Facts can be verified by examination of records in Source #8, looking under individual soldier's names. In some cases, additional personal information was derived from military pension records, Source #10, and these facts have also not been footnoted in every instance but are available from the National Archives, filed under the individual's name.*

2. *Illustrated History of New Mexico* (Chicago: Lewis Publishing Co., 1895), pp. 610–611.

3. Dorothy Kethler, "History of the Harwood Foundation," handout, Harwood Foundation, Taos, N.M. (1975).

4. "Mapa Historico de Taos," (Taos: Taos Press, n.d.) produced by Kiwanis Club of Taos.

5. Pension records, Sergeant David McAllister, Source #10.

6. Arrott Collection, Highlands University, Las Vegas, N.M.

7. Lt. Col. Wm. McMullen to Capt. Ben C. Cutler, March 16, 1864, Arrott Collection.

8. Ibid.

9. Post Returns, Fort Union, N.M., April, 1864, Arrott Collection.

10. S.O. 13, Dept. of N.M., Santa Fe, April 18, 1864, Source #7.

11. Brig. Gen. James H. Carleton to Brig. Gen. Lorenzo Thomas, April 17, 1864, Arrott Collection.

12. Ibid.

13. G.O. 12, Hqtrs., Dept. of N.M., Santa Fe, May 1, 1864, Arrott Collection.

14. Ibid.

15. Ibid.

16. Company A Muster Roll, December 31, 1863, Source #8.

17. Deposition by Capt. Smith Simpson, individual service record of Lt. Edward E. Ayer, Source #8.

18. S.O. 19, Dept. of N.M., Santa Fe, Source #8.

19. Fort Goodwin Post Returns, Aug., 1864, Source #9 and Lawrence Kelly, *Navajo Roundup* (Boulder, Colorado: The Pruett Publishing Co., 1970), p. 60.

20. *Official Report, War of the Rebellion,* Series 1, Vol. 50, Book 1 (Washington, D.C.: G.P.O., 1897), pp. 360–361.

21. G.O. 2, Hqtrs., Detach. of Apache Expedition, June 5, 1864, Source #7.

22. G.O. 1, Hqtrs., Detach. of Apache Expedition, June 4, 1864, Source #7.

23. S.O. 169, Hqtrs., Las Cruces, June 7, 1864, Source #7.

24. S.O. 3, Hqtrs., 4th District, Apache Expedition, Camp at Cienega, June 16, 1864, Source #7.

25. All members of the escort party have a notation, on their individual records in Source #8, that they made the trip.

26. *Official Report, War of the Rebellion,* Series 1, Vol. 50, Book 1, p. 364.

27. Ibid., p. 365.

28. Ibid.

29. *War of the Rebellion,* Series 1, Vol. 50, Book 1, p. 364.

30. Ibid.

31. Ibid., p. 367.

32. Brig. Gen. J. H. Carleton to Brig. Gen. L. Thomas, April 17, 1864, Arrott Collection.

33. G. O. 12, Hqtrs., Dept. of N.M., Santa Fe, May 1, 1864, Arrott Collection.

34. *War of the Rebellion,* Series 1, Vol. 50, Book 1, p. 368.

35. *War of the Rebellion,* Series 1, Vol. 41, Book 1, p. 82.

36. Ibid.

37. Ibid.

38. Ibid., p. 84.

39. Ibid.

40. Ibid.

41. Ibid.

42. *War of the Rebellion,* Series 1, Vol. 50, Book 1, p. 368.

43. *War of the Rebellion,* Series 1, Vol. 41, Book 1, p. 85.

44. *War of the Rebellion,* Series 1, Vol. 50, Book 1, p. 369.

45. *War of the Rebellion,* Series 1, Vol. 41, Book 1, p. 85.

46. Ibid., p. 86.

47. K. S. Woolsey to Gov. John H. Goodwin, Prescott, Ariz., Aug. 20, 1864, p. 18, Arizona Historical Society, Tucson.

48. *War of the Rebellion,* Series 1, Vol. 50, Book 1, pp. 368–370.

49. Ibid., p. 367.

50. Ibid., p. 370.

51. Company Muster Roll, July–August, 1864, Source #8.

52. Military Pension Records, Capt. S. Simpson, Source #10.

53. Ibid.

54. Ibid.

55. Ibid.

56. *War of the Rebellion,* Series 1, Vol. 41, Book 1, p. 82.

57. K. S. Woolsey to Gov. J. H. Goodwin, Prescott, Ariz., Aug. 20, 1864, p. 18.

58. *War of the Rebellion,* Series 1, Vol. 50, Book 1, p. 372.

59. Fort Goodwin Post Returns, Aug., 1864, Source #9.

60. Ibid.

61. Ibid.

62. Individual soldier's records, Source #8.

63. Post Returns, Fort Goodwin, Sept., 1864, Source #9.

64. Ibid.

65. *War of the Rebellion,* Series 1, Vol. 41, Book 3, p. 676.

66. *War of the Rebellion,* Series 1, Vol 41, Book 2, pp. 277–278.

67. *War of the Rebellion,* Series 1, Vol. 41, Book 3, pp. 851–852.

68. S.O. 190, Hqtrs., Fort Goodwin, Oct. 15, 1864, Source #7.

69. Fort Goodwin Post Returns, Nov., 1864, Source #9.

70. S.O. 213, Hqtrs., Fort Goodwin, Nov. 27, 1864, Source #7 and Fort Goodwin Post Returns, Nov., 1864, Source #9.

71. Herbert M. Hart, *Old Forts of the Far West* (Seattle: Superior Publishing Co., 1965), p. 81.

72. *War of the Rebellion,* Series 1, Vol. 50, Book 2, p. 1180.

73. Ibid.

74. S.O. 222, Hqtrs., Fort Goodwin, Dec. 8, 1864, Source #7.

75. Ind. record of Jose M. Casados, Source #8.

76. Fort Goodwin Post Returns, Dec., 1864, Source #9, and individual record of Antonio Meistes, Source #8.

77. Pension records, A. Meistes, Source #10.

78. *Santa Fe Weekly Gazette,* April 22, 1865.

79. *War of the Rebellion,* Series 1, Vol. 50, Book 1, p. 375.

80. Eugenio Romero Pension Records, Source #10.

81. Reyes Duran Pension Records, Source #10.

82. *War of the Rebellion,* Series 1, Vol. 50, Book 2, p. 1180.

83. Ibid.

84. Ralph Ogle, *Federal Control of the Western Apaches, 1848–1886* (Albuquerque: Univ. of N.M. Press, 1970), p. 58.

85. *Santa Fe Weekly Gazette,* April 22, 1865.

86. S.O. 192, Hqtrs., Ft. Union, N.M., Dec. 30, 1864, Source #7.

87. S.O. 13, Hqtrs., Ft. Goodwin, Source #7.

88. Ogle, *Federal Control of the Western Apaches, 1848–1886*, p. 51.

89. Fort Goodwin Post Returns, March, 1865, Source #9 and *Santa Fe Weekly Gazette*, April 22, 1865. The *Gazette* article set the number of Indians at 165. A letter, written by Major Gorman on April 5, 1865, *War of the Rebellion*, 1-50-2, p. 1180, sets the number at 112, confirming the Post Returns.

90. *War of the Rebellion*, Series 1, Vol. 50, Book 2, p. 1180.

91. *Santa Fe Weekly Gazette*, April 22, 1865.

92. *War of the Rebellion*, Series 1, Vol. 50, Book 2, p. 1180.

93. *Gazette*, April 22, 1865.

94. Ibid.

95. *War of the Rebellion*, Series 1, Vol. 48, Book 1, p. 1118 and *War of the Rebellion*, Series 1, Vol. 50, Book 2, p. 1180.

96. *War of the Rebellion*, Series 1, Vol. 50, Book 2, p. 1180.

97. S.O. 34, Hqtrs., Ft. Goodwin, Source #7.

98. *War of the Rebellion*, Series 1, Vol. 50, Book 2, p. 1180.

99. Ibid. Also see *Santa Fe Weekly Gazette*, April 8, 1865.

100. Fort Goodwin Post Returns, March, 1865, Source #9.

101. Jose R. Apodaca Individual Records, Source #8.

102. S.O. 43, Hqtrs., Fort Goodwin, Source #7.

103. Source #7.

104. S.O. 56, Hqtrs., Ft. Goodwin, May 16, 1865, Source #7.

105. Antonio J. Martin Individual Records, Source #8 and Fort Goodwin Post Returns, June, 1865, Source #9.

106. David McAllister Individual Records, Source #8.

107. William H. S. Bonsall Individual Record, Source #8.

108. Soldier's Individual Records, Source #8.

109. Fort Goodwin Post Returns, June, 1865, Source #9.

110. Hart, *Old Forts of the Far West*, p. 81.

111. Ibid.

112. S.O. 72, Hqtrs., Ft. Goodwin, July 2, 1865, Source #7 and S.O. 81, Hqtrs. Ft. Goodwin, July 19, 1865, Source #7.

113. S.O. 76, Hqtrs., Ft. Goodwin, Source #8.

114. S.O. 44, Hqtrs., Ft. Cummings, July 16, 1865, Source #2.

115. S.O. 46, Hqtrs. Ft. Cummings, July 25, 1865, Source #2.

116. Individual Records, Source #8.

117. S.O. 88, Hqtrs. Ft. Goodwin, Source #7.

118. S.O. 27, Hqtrs., Dist. of Arizona, Prescott, Source #7.

119. Ltr, #320, Brig. Gen. James Carleton to Gov. Henry Connelly, May 10, 1865, Arrott Collection.

120. Individual Record, Joseph Felmer, Source #8.

121. S.O. 95, Hqtrs. Ft. Goodwin, Source #7.

122. S.O. 104, Hqtrs. Ft. Goodwin, Source #7.

123. *War of the Rebellion*, Series 1, Vol. 50, Book 2, p. 1181 and *War of the Rebellion*, Series 1, Vol. 50, Book 1, p. 421–423.

124. Fort Goodwin Post Returns, November, 1865, Source #9.

125. Lt. Joseph Felmer to Lt. Col. Robert Pollock, Nov. 25, 1865, Source #7.

126. Ibid.

127. S.O. 133, Hqtrs., Fort Goodwin, Nov. 22, 1865, Source #7.

128. Ibid.

129. Letter of effects, April 25, 1866, Individual Record, Juan de Jesus Cordova, Source #8.

130. Individual Service Record, Smith Simpson, Source #8.

131. Ibid.

132. Ibid.

133. Ibid.

134. Ibid.

135. Ibid.

136. Ibid.

137. Ibid.

138. Brig. Gen. James Carleton to Gov. Henry Connelly, Aug. 19, 1865, Arrott Collection.

139. S.O. 60, Hqtrs., Dist of Arizona, Prescott, Nov. 16, 1865, Source #7.

140. Individual Service Record, James Mann, Source #8.

141. S.O. 11, Hqtrs., Ft. Goodwin, Feb. 14, 1866, Source #7.

142. Ibid.

143. S.O. 16, Hqtrs., Ft. Goodwin, Feb. 27, 1866, Source #7.

144. S.O. 19, Hqtrs., Ft. Goodwin, Source #7.

145. Fort Goodwin Post Returns, March, 1866, Source #9.

146. Fort Grant Post Returns, October, 1865, Source #3.

147. Fort Grant Post Returns, December, 1865, Source #3.

148. S.O. 33, Hqtrs. Ft. Goodwin, March 31, 1866, Source #7.

149. Fort Goodwin Post Returns, April, 1866, Source #9.

150. John C. Cremony, *Life Among the Apaches, 1850–1868* (San Francisco: A. Roman & Co., 1868)

93

reprinted ed. Glorieta, New Mexico: The Rio Grande Press, Inc., 1969, pp. 138–140.

151. Fort Grant Post Returns, April, 1866, Source #3.

152. Francis B. Heitman, *Historical Register and Dictionary of the United States Army, 1789–1903* (Washington: U.S. Government Printing Office, 1903) reprint ed., Urbana: Univ. of Illinois Press, 1967, p. 465.

153. Lori Davisson, Research Specialist, Arizona Historical Society, to Charles Meketa, Nov. 17, 1978.

154. Hart, *Old Forts of the Far West*, p. 81.

155. Fort Goodwin Post Returns, Source #9.

156. Ibid.

157. S.O. 40, Hqtrs., Ft. Goodwin, April 14, 1866, Source #7.

158. Order #51, Hqtrs, Ft. Goodwin, May 9, 1866, Source #7.

159. Ibid.

160. Order #52, Hqtrs., Ft. Goodwin, May 10, 1866, Source #7.

161. Order #54, Hqtrs., Ft. Goodwin, May 12, 1866, Source #7.

162. Order #59, Hqtrs., Ft. Goodwin, May 18, 1866, Source #7.

163. S.O. 61, Hqtrs., Ft. Goodwin, Source #7.

164. Fort Cummings Post Returns, June, 1866, Source #1.

165. Ibid.

166. Lt. Joseph Felmer to Major C. DeForrest, June 5, 1866, Felmer Individual Record, Source #8.

167. S.O. 17, Hqtrs., Dist of N.M., June 7, 1866, Source #7.

168. Col. Willis to Maj. C. DeForrest, June 24, 1866, Source #4 and S.O. 64, Hqtrs., Ft. Selden, N.M., June 21, 1866, Source #7.

169. S.O. 73, Hqtrs., Ft. Selden, Source #5.

170. S.O. 76, Hqtrs., Ft. Selden, July 22, 1866, Source #7.

171. S.O. 78, Hqtrs., Ft. Selden, Source #5.

172. S.O. 80, Hqtrs., Ft. Selden, Source #5.

173. S.O. 82, Hqtrs., Ft. Selden, Source #5.

174. Company I Muster Roll, July–Aug. 1866, Source #8.

175. *An illustrated History of New Mexico*, (Chicago, Lewis Publishing Co., 1895) p. 611 and "*History of the Harwood Foundation*," n.p.

176. "*History of the Harwood Foundation*," n.p.

177. Ibid.

178. Ibid.

179. Ibid.

180. Ibid.

181. Military Pension Records, Smith Simpson, Source #10.

182. *New Mexico Blue Book, 1882*, comp. W. G. Ritch (Albuquerque: Univ. of New Mexico Press, 1968), p. 113.

183. Pension Records, Source #10.

184. John Gregory Bourke, *On the Border with Crook* (New York: Charles Scribner's Sons, 1891) reprint ed., Glorieta, New Mexico: The Rio Grande Press, Inc., 1971, and Dan L. Thrapp, *The Conquest of Apacheria* (Norman: University of Oklahoma Press, 1967). See indexes of both books for frequent references to Felmer.

185. K. S. Woolsey to Gov. John H. Goodwin, Prescott, Ariz., Aug. 20, 1864, pp. 21–22, Arizona Historical Society, Tucson.

186. G.O. 12, Hqtrs., Dept. of N.M., May 1, 1864, Arrott Collection.

187. *War of the Rebellion*, Series 1, Vol. 41, Book 2, p. 278.

188. *War of the Rebellion*, Series 1, Vol. 50, Book 1, p. 374.

189. Ibid., p. 376.

190. Ibid., p. 377.

191. Ibid.

192. *War of the Rebellion*, Series 1, Vol. 50, Book 2, p. 1180.

193. Hart, *Old Forts of the Far West*, p. 82.

INDEX

95

97

99